# Number 2 Please

## The Story of a
# *Blind Date*
# Marriage

*Evelyn.*
*Best Wishes*

## David and Lilian Fensom

*Lilian & David.*

SUMMERSDALE

Summersdale Publishers
46 West Street
Chichester
West Sussex
PO19 1RP
United Kingdom

A CIP catalogue record for this book is available from
the British Library.

ISBN 1 873475 38 1

Printed and bound in Great Britain
by Selwood Printing Ltd., Burgess Hill.

# Acknowledgements

Cilla Black
and the London Weekend Television *Blind Date* Team
Lilian's and my Daughters
Interflora for Flowers
LWT for Flowers
Mike Vaughan, Photographer
Country Wedding Co. for cars
Jill and Robin Edmond
Susan McCulloch, Opera Singer
Queen's College Taunton for String Quartet
This Morning TV
Good Morning TV
Jane Asher and TV Weekly
Burnworthy Manor
Liz, Rupert & Waitresses
Rhona Gillmore
Judith Goss
Travel Lodge, Tiverton
Neil Rice, Hairdresser, Liverpool
Birmingham Jewellery Quarter
Jersey Tourism
Hotel L'Horizon
Europcar
Jersey European Airways
P. & O. Cruises
Margaret Beadle & Jersey Battle of Flowers Association
Tony Hardman

Mid Devon District Council
Eggesford House Hotel, Fox & Hounds
Rev. Tony Grosse
Registrar @ Tiverton
Church Choir & Bellringers
Ushers
Tiverton & Hemyock Police
Flower Ladies at Church
Guests at Wedding
Wellwishers gathered at Tiverton
Wellwishers gathered at Hemyock
The Press
Everybody who wrote to us
Everybody who spoke to us

## Dedication

This book is dedicated to Cilla and Bobby, to the Director, Producer, Researchers, and all members of the Production Team on the *Blind Date* television show, without whom this book would not have been written.

We also include both Lilian's and my daughters and their families. Without their support we would not have embarked on this enterprise.

# Contents

# Chapter 1

## Introduction

**Lilian**

Hello, let me introduce myself: I am Lilian, the other half of Lilian and David, of Cilla Black's *Blind Date* Wedding, the second wedding in the ten year history of the show. *Wow*, what a wedding! But first let us start at the beginning.

On the First of July 1922 at a Hospital in Newcastle-upon-Tyne, Lilian Weatherburn made her debut followed at intervals by a sister Eleanor then a brother Raymond and lastly another brother William Martin. I enjoyed my childhood where I lived in Watson Street, Walker, had a super time as a teenager, then joined the WAAF when I was nineteen.

I served four years during World War II, at West Drayton, Middlesex, attaining the rank of Corporal. I married an airman from the same station, and when demobbed set up home in Liverpool, where I stayed for forty years - hence my Geordie and Scouse accents.

At the age of sixty two I divorced and decided to go
it alone, and vowed that I would never marry again:
but then of course we never know what fate has in
store for us, do we? The next nine years were spent
dancing, partying and having fun, and during this
period I moved back to my home town of Newcastle,
into sheltered accommodation, Grasmere House,
Walker, where for four years I helped to run the Bingo,
raffles etc., made some good friends and really enjoyed
my life, which included voluntary work in the charity
shop of the British Heart Foundation. Considering
myself to be fun loving and game for a laugh, I wrote
to the *Blind Date* Television Studios, and duly received
an application form.

The response to my application was a request that I
attend for audition at an hotel in Newcastle, so off I
went. There were lots of us including many students,
all hoping for a 'Blind Date'. We girls were interviewed
four at a time by a lovely young lady named Isobel
who seemed very impressed by my age, and paid me a
nice compliment by saying that I had lovely legs. This
was in February 1993.

I must have scored good marks or something because
the postman delivered a large envelope with
instructions to attend a second audition at an hotel.
This time it was to be in Edinburgh, and I was
delighted. What a wonderful fun day we all had there.
In my group there were eleven of us ladies all doing
our party piece, so it was a laugh from beginning to

end. We were chosen at random to stand up and talk about ourselves for ten minutes or so in front of the panel of interviewers. We answered questions about ourselves and our reasons for wanting to appear on the show, etc.

We were given two questions on a paper, and were asked to think up our answers during a ten minute break with refreshments. Put into groups of four, a young man, Mike, stood behind our chairs, introduced himself, numbered us one to four (myself being number three) then asked us the first question. Of course, we were not permitted to refer to any notes we might have made, but had to rely on our memories or spontaneous wit, whatever.

The first question was, 'My children can't keep up with me as I'm too fast for them. How would you keep up with me, Number Three?' My reply, 'Well, Mike, I take vitamins every day, and anything you can do I can do better,' earned me some applause.

His second question, 'My children are studying statistics at school. What do you know about them, Number Three?'

'I don't know anything about them, only my own vital ones, thirty-six, twenty-six, thirty-eight.'

Mike jumped in the air, saying, 'Wow! If you're telling the truth, Number Three, you have a fantastic figure.' So cheeky Number Three put her hands on her hips, stood up and said,

'Would you like me to prove it?'

I must say that I had applause from the panel and my fellow contestants. I thoroughly enjoyed the whole audition, felt very happy with myself, and I cannot speak too highly of the television crew and their kindness and ability to put us, the potential contestants, completely at ease.

After minor formalities, taking our photograph etc., we left for home, having been advised to act as normal, and told that if chosen for the show we would be informed, and if not, that we could apply the following year.

Lucky for me, I had a telephone call from Isobel to ask if I was still interested in the show. You can imagine my joy and eager 'yes', especially when she told me that I would be a 'picker'. Gosh! I was thrilled and telephoned family and friends. Most were happy for me, but my daughter Linda who lived in Liverpool wasn't very happy about it, and said she would not watch it when it came on the screen, and she didn't!

My boss at the charity shop where I worked, Janice, and all my friends were delighted for me, so when a strapless evening dress came into the shop they insisted on dressing me up in it, saying it would be perfect for the Blind Date, so I bought it. Black satin overlaid with purple lace. I also had evening culottes, black pleated trousers, and a gold and blue satin top. I would be taking both outfits to the show, the final decision as to what I should wear would be taken after camera shots. The big day was now not far away.

## David

This is me, David, born in Fife, Scotland in 1923. I spent most of my life in Essex, where I was educated in Hornchurch, and then employed initially in Naval Architecture until I entered into the Royal Navy in 1942. I served four years principally on Tank Landing Craft as a Petty Officer, and was demobbed in 1946, returning to civilian life and the Drawing Office. Engineering design and sales took up a large portion of my life.

I had married during the war years, and now had two daughters. I became involved as a volunteer with a local branch of the Samaritans, which took up a large portion of my spare time. From that I was accepted for training for the then *Marriage Guidance Counsel* (now *Relate*). After twenty years in one company I became redundant and joined a small new engineering company, with which I was very much engrossed in my work, and from which I retired when I reached sixty five.

In my early fifties, through no fault of my wife's, we parted and divorced, and I married again soon after, cancer taking my second wife from me in 1992. I had moved to the West Country upon retirement, and being on my own, moved in with my daughter Georgina and her family. Georgina made several suggestions as to how I could occupy myself, but to no avail, they fell on deaf ears. However, full marks for effort, she spotted an article in the local paper which

stated that auditions were being held in an hotel in
Taunton for Cilla Black's *Blind Date* show. She
suggested that I might go along.

What, me? On the Cilla Black show? Not likely! At
first, I dismissed the idea completely out of hand: why
on earth would they want a seventy year old man to
appear on this popular Saturday evening show, at peak
viewing time, dominated principally by fresh faced
youngsters, full of fun, laughter, *Coca-cola* and devil-
may-care attitudes? The men, many fresh out of
college, witty, dashing, crowd-drawing and keen. And
the women, sleek, beautiful, charming, a twinkle in their
eyes, with the bloom of youth in their cheeks and the
cheeks of . . . well, you know the rest.

Now, how could an old chap like me fit in with
that lot? I asked myself. I knew that I had seen golden
oldies before on the shows, and I must admit that I
had admired their guts and nerve, and enjoyed the
spectacle, which prompted me to think that love was
perhaps not just for the young, but for all who were
young at heart.

My resistance to presenting myself for an audition
was beginning to weaken. Maybe in some small way I
could contribute something if I had the chance, maybe
I could summon up that hidden part of me that lies
dormant in most of us. The magic of television, the
endless possibilities of entertainment. Why not? I had
now passed from the definite *No* stage on to the *Maybe*
stage. It was now up to me to take the final step. After

all it was no big deal, I wouldn't get through the first stage, of that I was convinced, so why all this fuss? Exit one would-be star of the future, down at the first fence. But there again, that's no way to take up a challenge, it's all or nothing.

The vision of all that I had just mentioned flashed before me, and I thought that if I didn't try now, I never would. There are many times in my life that I had stuck my neck out; the faint-hearted do not prosper in this world. Decisions! Decisions! Isn't that what life is all about? It's how we carry them out, and how we come through them that matters. In for a penny, in for a pound. So I said, 'Oh, alright then!'

Having made this momentous decision, the question of what to wear arose, and so it was off to Exeter, where the magic plastic took a bashing, and on the chosen day, I presented myself, along with dozens of other hopefuls, at the rendezvous.

Now, I have always believed that first impressions count, be it applying for a job, visiting a customer for a contract, or a friend for a meal. Consequently I wore the new duds that I had recently acquired. However, I must admit I had second thoughts about that when I entered the waiting room, I might have felt more at ease in a pair of jeans and a tee shirt with 'I'm a Pratt' printed across it. But I consoled myself that this was really me, and my confidence was not impaired. In fact I had a boost when a good looking young lady entered the room, asked me if I were the producer,

and what did she have to do to audition for the show?
I must admit a naughty thought crossed my mind, but
I said, 'Take a ticket, fill in a form and sit down and
wait with all of us contestants.'

After a while we were called in groups, one of men,
the other of women, to sit at a table, with a charming
young woman. It was a getting-to-know-you thing,
we all chatted at random with her and with each other,
speaking generally about ourselves, why we were keen
to go on the show. It was a very enjoyable discussion:
she had the knack of prompting us to respond in the
way she wanted.

Having achieved what I thought was a slim chance
of selection, bearing in mind the great number of
applicants and the obvious abundance of potential
talent that was there, I returned home thinking that at
least I had tried.

Imagine my surprise when some weeks later I had a
letter from LWT inviting me to a second audition on
the 12th May at an hotel, this time in Bristol. Hell's
Bell's I was in for another chance to be on the big
show. I remember that day very well. There was a
bomb scare in the city, and a sizeable chunk of the
shopping precinct had been cordoned off and
evacuated. Fortunately, the hotel for which I was
heading was on the outer fringe of the 'no go' area,
and was seething with police and others holding
meetings and discussions.

I can picture the audition now, a long table with producer, researchers and team members sat with their documents, in front of us. Again we were asked individually to talk about ourselves, followed by a mock *Blind Date* question set-up. Having been given a couple of questions, we had to memorise our own answers, then a few minutes later, put into groups of three or four, and given a number. We sat in a group of three with a young lady behind us to ask the questions, which we did when our number was called. My favourite question was, 'Men like my knobbly knees, what do women like about you?'

Now for this I had to stand to act my answer which was, 'Women like my squinty eyes, my wooden leg and my humpty back, apart from which they dislike me intensely.' And I must admit to feeling pleased when I had some applause.

After formalities, photographs being taken of us individually, etc., I departed, with a feeling of having given it my best shots, and it now lay in the laps of the Gods as to the outcome.

Time passed, and then, out of the blue, a telephone call was answered by my young Granddaughter who said, 'Grandpa, it's for you, Isobel from the Television.' Yes, she asked if I were still interested in appearing on the show, and when I answered 'yes' she told me that I would be one of three men on the stools. Yippee! I was on!

# Chapter 2

## The Show

### Lilian's View

The big day arrived, the 11th October 1993. Feeling very excited, I waited for the taxi to take me to the railway station, to board a train bound for Kings Cross. My Warden, Dot Allen, of Grasmere House, was waiting to wish me good luck along with two of my friends Emma and Margaret: after hugs and waves I was on my way into the unknown. As it was many years since I had visited London, I was unsure of my way around. I therefore decided to take a taxi direct to the LWT studios. With butterflies in my tummy, it was 2.00 pm when I arrived, but my appointment was for 3.30 pm, not a minute later or a minute before, were the instructions.

I was now in a quandary as to what to do. It was a lovely sunny day so I decided to sit on a wall outside the studios and wait, but then I began to feel foolish so I strode in through the main door to the reception, introduced myself and apologised for my early arrival.

The receptionist kindly suggested that I left my suitcase behind the desk, which incidentally was very heavy and held everything except the proverbial kitchen sink, and that I could pop up the road to a cafe. I waited there until the time arrived for me to present myself back at reception, whereupon I was met by Annetta from the *Blind Date* team.

We next met my stand-by, Pearl, and Eddie the other picker and his stand-by. The stand-bys are necessary to understudy in the event of non-arrival, stage fright or illness etc: thankfully unnecessary in our cases. We attended a run through of what was expected of us, and held up our two proposed outfits in front of the camera, whereupon the producer Thelma McGough and others of the team decided which would be most suitable for the show.

After a meal Pearl and I were allocated a shared dressing room, and there hanging up were my outfits, with a note on the black and purple which said 'Lilian, wear this'. After washing and dressing, it was necessary for me to visit the ladies' room. As I was walking along the corridor, a door opened and out came Thelma. She spotted me and said, 'Lilian, you look fabulous.'

Behind her then appeared Cilla, saying, 'You look gorgeous, Lilian,' and then guess what? Bobby looked out for a glimpse of this vision, all I could say was, 'Oh, Cilla.' It was such a surprise. Annetta took Eddie and myself to the hairdresser and make-up department. Eddie, a lovely lad with a bald head and a terrific personality received attention first due to his appearance on the first part of the show. We had lots of laughs with him, particularly when he asked make-up to shine his bald head.

Whilst undergoing my 'beauty treatment' it was possible to watch the show on a monitor, and Eddie's was a super performance, choosing Donna from Rochdale, another great performer.

My big moment was getting closer, Annetta was escorting me through the seemingly endless corridors, dodging about to ensure no bumping into male contestants! Fortunately we did not, as it is not allowed until after the meetings on stage.

While Cilla was chatting to my three men, I was sat behind the scenery wearing headphones and listening to music, so I had no knowledge of the conversations that she was having with them. Cilla came to see me to be sure that I was alright, and put me entirely at ease by saying that I looked fabulous. My pulse quickened as Chris O'Dell took me by the hand and led me to the steps, again saying, 'Are you alright?'

He then explained that when Cilla calls, 'Come on in, Lilian,' I was to walk forward, stop on the green cross, and, remembering that there are two hundred people watching in the audience, (but he never mentioned the millions of people that would be watching on their television screens) I was to smile and wave from left to right, sweeping across to take them all in. This I did and got carried away with the applause, picking up the hem of my dress and curtsying. The audience roared their approval and Cilla said 'Ooh-er' and laughed.

If you have short legs like mine you will know how difficult it is to get up on one of those high stools. I had mentioned at rehearsal about falling off, but they laughed and said that I wouldn't. Well I did, my foot slipped and Cilla put her hand out to save me. I didn't really make a mess of it but nevertheless felt a bit of a fool. Cilla asked where I worked, and I said that it was in a charity shop in Wallsend-on-Tyne (I can mention in this book that it is the British Heart Foundation) and when asked what was sold in the shop I replied, 'Clothes,' then I lifted my skirt and said, 'hence the dress, but the jewels are mine.'

Here I am now, sat on this high stool with three questions which I have to ask the three invisible gentlemen. I will say here that I was asked to submit a total of twelve questions, from which would be selected the considered best three, and here they are: -

**Number One**
I do French maid kissograms to raise money for charity and I must admit that I do love putting on fancy dress, so which outfit would most turn you on?

**Number Two**
I'm very emotional and cry all the way through sad movies, and when the lights go up in the cinema I have huge red eyes. What would you do to cheer me up?

### Number Three

Although I'm seventy one, I'm young at heart and love to sneak a go on the children's swings and slides. What's your favourite ride in the playground and why?

As the gentlemen were answering my questions I was saying to myself, 'He sounds nice, I must remember him,' but I am afraid that as soon I started to read the next question, I had already forgotten who answered what. Even when Number Two sang 'Any Old Iron' and we sang along with him, and we all had a good laugh, I didn't make a mental note. It all goes on so quickly, it's difficult to collect one's thoughts.

But here was 'our Graham' with the reminders, and as he finished speaking, I said to Cilla, 'Number Two please.'

As the applause for Graham died down, Cilla said to me, 'Well Lilian you just whispered to me but no one else heard it so you'd better repeat it.'

I said it now in a loud voice, '**NUMBER TWO PLEASE!**'

By the sound of the applause, I gathered that the audience thought that I had made the right choice. However, after Vic and Norman had left the set, I was hoping that I had made the best choice, the screen moved away and then I saw David . . . I turned to Cilla and said, 'Oh Cilla, he has a beard and I hate whiskers,' to which Cilla replied,

'Well, you'll have to get him to shave it off, Chuck.'

When David came forward to kiss me I gave him a look which said 'You're a bit of alright!'

Standing either side of Cilla, I picked the card from her hand: we had a date in Jersey. I felt so happy, neither David or myself had been to Jersey, the 'Honeymoon Island', before. We thanked Cilla and left the set holding hands. Arriving backstage the young contestants complimented, hugged and kissed us. Then the finale for the evening meant that we all sat on the sofa, where Cilla joined us and we waved to the audience, and of course, the viewers.

As we left the stage one of the girls shouted, 'Look at David, he's still holding Lilian's hand!'

Then David put his other hand on top of mine and said, 'Yes, and I don't intend to let go.'

Wasn't that lovely? I felt so thrilled. Looking back on all that excitement, I know that he is still holding my hand.

Now it was upstairs to the hospitality room for champagne and a sandwich. David phoned his daughter and told her that he had been chosen, and was off to Jersey with a woman named Lilian. He seemed very excited.

I enjoyed the evening with them all, most of them being youngsters who looked upon us as the 'Golden Oldies', being in our early seventies, but I am sure they liked us. Now, sitting at the opposite end of our table was my Number Three, Norman from London, and every time I lifted my glass our eyes met, and he appeared to be forlorn and miserable - I believe he wished that I had chosen him. I said to him, 'Norman, how about you giving me your address, and I'll drop you a line?' As I was saying this David, who had just returned from the bar, and I didn't know was behind me, said, 'How about that, she's my date and she's planning to write to someone else.' Well, in fact I did write eventually to him, but it was from both of us, and it was to invite him to our wedding.

We had a great time with them all, but we had to go, as the taxi was waiting for us, so it was goodbye, and we were off to the hotel near Gatwick where we were to spend the night. Three of the *Blind Date* team accompanied us, and although it was after midnight when we arrived a buffet supper was laid on. It was late when we retired to our rooms.

After a six o'clock early morning call, and a quick bath we were off to the airport. I rang my daughter, who was delighted to hear the good news. I was on a high, my feet weren't touching the ground, and I was swept along on what for me was a great adventure. Would I wake up and find that it was only a dream? No, David was here beside me, and guess what? He was still holding my hand. I think I'll give him a chance to have his say.

# The Show

**David's View**

To appear on television for the first time in one's life is an experience not to be taken lightly, and from the layman's point of view can be traumatic in the extreme. The anticipation is exciting, coupled with a certain amount of trepidation. But the elation overcomes the fear, the adrenaline starts pumping, and the whole of the mind is geared up and concentrated on this great occurrence which is now about to happen.

Well, that's how I see it anyway, but to many I am sure it is just one of those happenings that you drift in and out of, and which makes no real mark or effect on the journey through life. Maybe it's because I am seventy plus, and all those experiences which I passed through during those years, and many of which, if not all, registered in my mind and affected my journey through time, including my part in the D-Day landings.

I was then the Motor Mechanic in charge of the engines in a Tank Landing Craft, number 1014, my battle station being at the controls of the two 600 HP Diesels, the fumes of which became a fog, and the noise was deafening. We were fortunate that we survived the initial onslaught on that day, June 6th, and went on to make many more trips between Britain and France, bringing men, tanks and equipment. Eventually it became impossible to pump the sea water from the leaking hull fast enough to remain afloat, and she found her last resting place in Devon. I then joined a similar vessel, the 11001 bound for the Far East, only to reach Egypt, to find myself on a troopship bound for home. It was whilst on this troopship that the ship's Captain broadcast a message to us all that the Japanese had capitulated, the war was over!

But all this was a long time ago, and upon reflection I do not think it had such an impact or change in my lifestyle as that which was about to evolve.

Of course I had no idea as to what lay ahead, although I regularly watched the programme and am a great fan of Cilla. All I knew was that I had to sit on a stool, chat to Cilla, and answer three questions from an unknown person behind a partition on the stage. I hoped that in some way, if they were witty enough, that I, whose name had been substituted by a number between one to three, could convince that person that I was the most suitable person to be with on a date, to goodness knows where. Like millions of others, I had sat and watched the show on a Saturday evening, in a comfortable chair with a cup of coffee or a glass of wine, and eagerly awaited the arrival of the three who would emerge and sit, in the case of the men, a little ungainly on the high stools.

I still watch the show, with my wife, and we decide between us who we think would be the best partner for the 'picker', be it male or female. There are many that I can remember, especially those who were on the same show as myself, and who appear in the 'on the sofa' photographs on my lounge wall. I digress and must return to my feelings about the show, because now I knew that I was to be watched rather than watching, that a woman was going to ask me to reply to her questions. What was she going to be like? Was she tall, short, large or small? From where would she come, and, very importantly, if I were fortunate enough to be chosen, would I like her, and would she like me?

What kind of questions is this lady of hitherto unknown origin and appearance going to ask of us three, to which we must find a suitable answer? We had to be humorous, but not too naughty, to think of answers which would make our audience laugh, and delight our millions of viewers, to incite them to leap out of their chairs shouting 'pick him, pick him!'. I knew that somehow my efforts and projection of myself in that short period were all that I had, and that I must do my damndest to win that prize, a date with a Doll at the television company's expense. How on earth could I have foretold the outcome of my future after the most momentous events which were about to unfold?

These feelings and thoughts were in my mind, and I now had a definite date of Monday 11th of October 1993. I was to arrive at the studios at a precise time, which I rightly construed was to ensure that I did not bump into anybody else personally appearing on the show which might cause any embarrassment or complication. Ah! Now things became a little tricky: I had been advised that certain clothing can cause problems with the televised picture, creating a flaring, strobing and 'washed-out' appearance. In consequence, I decided on another trip to make use of the magic plastic.

How would we manage today in this new world of computerisation without this all-knowing, all-powerful little strip of plastic? Would we have to shop with our pockets bulging with banknotes or cheque books? Have you ever been stuck in a supermarket check-out and frantically searched through plastic cards which will buy you a tin of paint in every do-it-yourself shop in the country, and find that the one you need is the one in your other jacket at home? Having got that off my chest, I'll return to the matter in hand.

I required clothing that was neither black nor white nor pastel coloured, not with fine stripes or small checks. Everything else was fine, so I was informed. It did cross my mind that if I walked into my favourite shop in Exeter and asked for a suit that was not black nor white nor pastel coloured nor striped nor checked, I might expect to get a suitable answer. I could even end up being escorted to the door by two in blue, or, heaven forbid, in white. What am I talking about? Oh yes, I did get fixed up with suitable attire in the end. In case I was lucky enough to get picked, I had to take with me suitable clothing for hot and cold climates, a swimming costume and a ten year passport (What a long date this could be, I must return before the ten years are up). Many friends and relatives rang me and wished me luck, and I was told that all my old workmates would be rooting for me.

So, the day arrived and I took the train to London, lugging a bulging suitcase, with a spring in my step and a feeling of great elation. I arrived bang on time at the studio. So far, so good. I was met at reception, taken up lifts and escorted through seemingly endless corridors and finally arrived, along with Vic and Norman and our stand-by at our dressing room. Now we produced the two outfits each, and were taken to the set, dangled them in front of us while the technicians decided what we would wear in front of the cameras. As soon as the decision was made, they were whisked off to be 'pressed' and upon return to the dressing room, there they were all ready for us.

I find that in large buildings with lots of floors and corridors I need a guide to enable me to re-trace my steps, should I, for example, wish to visit the men's room, which invariably means a few left and right hand turns. I favour a reel of cotton, I presume a similar process when potholing, but it is rather impractical, and should many do this, the whole building would eventually give the appearance of a badly knitted string vest.

You will by now have reached the conclusion that my sense of direction is roughly zero. For example, if

I park my car in a supermarket car park, it is usually wiser on my part to take two bearings, in order to line up the spot where I left it. But you know how it is, I only went in for a few items, and left an hour later with a trolley fully laden with bags of shopping, hadn't bothered to take my bearings, and find myself stupidly walking up and down the rows trying to locate my vehicle. Coupled with which my trolley has been invariably programmed to take its own zig zag course. I believe that somebody has now designed a trolley which will respond to the direction desired by the pusher. Good show! I once had a trolley, laden with paving slabs which would only travel in circles whilst in the store, much to the amusement of my fellow shoppers. Well, if it gives some people a laugh, there's no harm done.

Don't worry, Reader, the wedding is in this book, I promise.

As my new-found colleagues and I were to be on the second part of the show, we watched the first part on a monitor in a back room. Then it was off to make-up for a dash of powder on our faces and a general scrutiny before the appearance. There was one more bridge to cross, however. We were given a paper which described the three questions we were about to be asked, told to scribble our answers, show them to the writer for his approval, and then had to remember them, as no referring is to be allowed. This process takes only a few minutes, and it is surprising how quickly a humorous answer can come to mind.

We approached the back of the set. Cilla was talking, referring to the 'three lovely lads' and saying, 'Come on in, Vic from Bournemouth, David from Devon and Norman from London.'

A voice whispered, 'Quickly now, you're on,' and we three walked onto the set. Can you imagine it? You don't have to, because you've probably, like me, seen it dozens of times, but to me, appearing for the very first time in my life in front of what would be millions of viewers, it was a moment that I shall never forget. I felt as if I was going to be blindfolded and shot. Gee! was it hot under the lights: dimly in the distance I could glimpse the two hundred or so in the live audience. But what excitement! A thought flashed into my mind: did I do up the zip in my trousers? Obviously I had because they did not stop the show to put matters right.

This was the point where Cilla put us at our ease, chatting to us one at a time. When it came to my turn, she referred to me as Colonel Sanders (I wonder if KFC would give me a job?). I had never attained the promotion to Colonel, principally because the Royal Navy does not have such a rank, and in my modest way I had only reached Petty Officer. Nevertheless, I assume etiquette would require a Colonel to salute a lady when addressed by one, and so I did. The introductions complete, Cilla returned to the stage and called, 'Come on in Lilian.'

Now all the questions I had wondered about came flooding back, and I tried to paint a mental picture of this lady behind the screen. She was a Geordie all right, there was no mistaking that accent, and a cheeky one too. How many women at seventy-one do French Maid Kissograms? Not many, I'll wager.

She mentioned the kissograms and asked what I would have her wear to turn me on? Vic and Norman when asked talked about the can-can and the frilly knickers, and I said that it would be composed of three first class postage stamps, strategically placed, which would give me a mail advantage. I won't comment on that except to say that I have never seen such a costume and probably never will. Pity!

Lilian's second question was about crying at sad movies and what would we do to cheer her up? I'm afraid that I went over the top on this one and said that I might sing 'Any Old Iron', but that it might make her worse, and did she want to hear it? The audience, bless them, shouted 'yes', so I asked if Lilian wanted to hear it. Cilla peeped round the wall and said, 'Yes, she does.' Now I had committed myself, the world's second worst singer (dear Arthur Mullard being in my estimation the number one) to singing on stage in front of millions of viewers. I knew that there would be no record contracts for me, no groups clamouring for me to appear at their concerts, no Royal

Variety performances, no shrieking fans chucking their underwear at me to mop my brow. But in spite of all this, you may ask what made me make a spectacle of myself? I have asked myself the same question. Was it the sheer audacity of it? Was it taking advantage of an opportunity that could never happen again? Was I trying to prove something to myself?

Let me explain something, when I was a lad we had the then traditional round of parties with relatives and friends, at any conceivable occasion, and who was the one who was always doing the conjuring tricks, singing the songs, of which he knew many? It was my Dad. As a young man and a scoutmaster at the time, he told me that he once sang on the stage with Bud Flanagan, and I believe him. It was he who pushed me off that stool. My Dad, my friend.

I can remember hearing Lilian say, 'Very nice,' and wondered if she would remember that it was me when it would come for her to make her choice. Most probably not, it would create another confusion in her brain. We, the men, had only to give three answers each, but she would have to listen to nine, then make her judgement after Graham had given his reminders. Maybe the last question is the most significant one that can influence the choice, who knows? But I think I would rather be where I am, with a one in three chance of selection, than having to make that decision.

I know that we are the puppets in a very popular game show which has huge credit worthiness and television appeal, especially as the presenter, Cilla Black, is surely the best and most loved game show presenter in the business today. Lilian and I say that, not just because she has done so much for us personally and we are very fond of her and her husband Bobby, but because we believe it is true.

Yes! I did mention that we are puppets in a game, but most of us give of our best. Together with Cilla we make the programme, for a short while we hold the stage, then afterwards disappear back into our own normality. But while on the show we each bring with us our feelings, excitement, exhilaration, happiness, sadness and disappointment.

Don't put this book down, I haven't mentioned the last of Lilian's questions. She said that she sneaked rides in children's playgrounds, what ride would we prefer, and why? Vic said the swings, up and down, up and down, up and down, and accompanied it with the gestures. Then Norman, when it was his turn, preferred to ride a piggy back, with Lilian as his horse. Mine was on the mat with Lilian on the helter skelter, finishing up entwined at the bottom.

Phew! The questions and answers were over, Graham gave his spiel, so who would it be? The three of us sat there with bated breath. Lilian spoke -

'Number two please.'

Without wishing to sound dramatic, these three spoken words were the turning point in my life. How could I possibly foretell what lay ahead? My head was in a whirl, my big moment was about to come. I had been excited from the start, but this was something else, and after Vic and Norman had departed sadly from the scene, it was time for the screen to roll away, and there she was, my Date, Lilian.

Picking the envelope from Cilla's hand is usually done by the female. It's either because the male considers it to be the gentlemanly gesture for the lady to have the freedom of choice, or that it precludes the male from making a decision on the inevitable outcome, if you see what I mean? I cannot help wondering sometimes as to where the other envelopes would have sent us? One had already gone to the previous couple on the set. I would hasten to add that for us it was the perfect place to go on a date, to the romantic island of Jersey. Neither of us had visited the island before, but I must confess that for many years I had wished to go. Yes! It was the ideal place for us both. We chatted with Cilla, thanked her, and left the set holding hands.

I had made it, the impossible had happened, the agony of decisions over, the excitement of the auditions successfully accomplished, and the lady had chosen me, and what a great lady she appeared to be. It was a bit like those magazine competitions when you are advised that you have come through the preliminary rounds, and you are now down for the big one. The big one had certainly come up in my case, it was now up to me, and of course to my lady date also, as to what each of us would make of it. For my part, I had taken an instant liking to Lilian, I was captivated by her charm, her wit, her complete personality. Boy, was I the lucky one! I was floating on air, it was no wonder that I was to fall in love with her.

The show closes with all the performers in that evening's show gathered around the sofa with Cilla, waving to the audience and the viewers. For us, it was up to the hospitality room after changing and gathering our gear. I had time for a quick call home with the good news. Hugs and kisses and congratulations all round, and a glass or two of champagne, before hearing the words,

'Lilian and David, your taxi is here.' So now we were off to the Copthorne Hotel, near Gatwick, on our way. It was late when we arrived, however, food was made available to us, for which we were thankful, and it was off to our rooms, together with our television crew who would be accompanying us, as we all had an early call. It was an early flight.

# Chapter 3

## The Date

A six o'clock early morning call had been booked for both of us. There was time for a quick shower before we met in the foyer, followed by a taxi to the airport, then check-in. Breakfast was arranged, Lilian had time for a telephone call to her daughter Linda in Liverpool, telling her that she had picked me, David, that I seemed to be a nice fellow, and that we were off to Jersey. Linda said,

'Lucky you, I've always wanted to go there. Have a good time.'

Next Lilian rang her very good friend Belle to give her the good news, and she said that she was delighted, good for her, enjoy herself, and if she were not too busy, to give her another ring to let her know how it was all going. Lilian did just that, that very evening, both of us in the phone booth, me feeding in the coins, while she introduced us to each other on the blower. Lilian said that Belle's reaction was 'Ooh er! he sounds smashing, I like his voice,' to which Lilian replied 'That's why I said number two please.'

After breakfast, and a wait in the V. I. P. lounge, we were greeted by the stewardess as we boarded the plane, and she ushered us to the two forward seats. While it was great to be given a small bottle of champagne each, with the compliments of the airline, looking around I noticed that we were the only ones drinking champagne. The champers fuelled the excitement as we arrived over land and touched down on the tarmac.

Upon leaving the plane, the stewardess took Lilian's arm and whispered in her ear 'I can see you chose the right one.' Now Lilian's thoughts were, how would she know? The show hadn't yet been televised. She must have thought that we were well suited, and that David was the right one for her, irrespective of whoever the other contestants might have been. If these were her thoughts, then she was perfectly right.

I must excuse myself for being a little hazy as to who picked up the baggage, because there, waiting at the door, was a chauffeur driven limousine. An excellent time, I thought, to give Lilian a kiss, which I proceeded to do, oblivious to the round of applause coming from the watching television crew. There followed a tour around parts of the island, our driver explaining interesting features as we approached them. He also told us the car we were in was the one which Her Majesty the Queen Mother had used during visits to the island, and that the actor John Nettles, 'Bergerac', had also frequently used it on his visits.

We arrived at the hotel, *L'Horizon* in St Brelade, to be greeted and welcomed by the Manager. We were shown to our rooms, beautifully appointed and overlooking the sea. By this time the television crew had arrived at the hotel having off-loaded the camera gear from the plane, and into a van. This van would subsequently be tailing us during our planned excursions. We were both amazed at the amount of equipment necessary to record the events of the date, box upon box.

The itinerary had been well prepared: first stop, the Jersey Potteries. A portion of the workshop had been taped off, and, watched by a curious crowd, I had to don a white smock, and closely follow the actions of the potter at his wheel. I was told that I was expected to produce a similar pot to the one he had just made . . . well, it looked quite simple, really. The first objective was to chuck the lump of squashy wet clay bang into the centre of the rotating wheel. Number one fault, I missed the centre, and the confidence with which I had been oozing began to wane, as the only oozing was the wobbling mass between my busy fingers. Not to be deterred however, I *pottered* on. Thank goodness for the smock, otherwise I might have spent the rest of the day looking as if I had been careless over lunch. Now the masterpiece which I was creating began to get a little out of hand, causing me to deposit quite large amounts of the clay into the sink, leaving me with a small muddy wet lump about the size of a golf ball. But was I beaten? Contrary to common belief, I considered that there was still enough material to create a somewhat smaller edition of the model. Feeling quite proud of my efforts, I stood back to accept the tumultuous applause, but sad to say the only reaction I got was when Lilian referred to my pot as a pixie's egg cup. Shame! I think that it was at that precise moment my thoughts of a profession in the future as a Master Potter were terminated. Laugh, of course we all did, and I chuckle every time I glimpse the object in the cabinet. Does anybody know a pixie who would like an egg cup?

After visiting the shop, followed by a coffee break, we both toured the pottery exhibits, little knowing that we would be coming back here in the not-too-distant future. Upon leaving, we were both given a memento of our visit, a small bowl crafted in the workshops. We bade farewell, our next visit, the zoo.

On arrival and having been greeted by our host, we were invited to tour the zoo seated on the back of a small motor driven buggy, much like the ones golfers use to get around the course. This turned out to be the golden opportunity for Lilian and I to get really friendly, clutching on to each other with one hand and the other on to the seat to prevent us both pitching *base over apex* off the back.

It was a most exciting journey between the animal pens as our driver, bless him, appeared not to be aware of where the paths lay, but took the crow's route from one destination to another. I took the opportunity afforded by this somewhat intimate occasion to give Lilian another kiss, an event which I believe appealed favourably to us both. She certainly didn't push me off the back or protest loudly. I think perhaps she was too scared or afraid that she might fall, and another way of hanging on, as both hands were occupied, was by the mouth! Novel, eh?

At one stage we were standing alongside the gorilla's cage, fortunately separated from the onlookers by a glass wall, possibly an inch or so thick. Suddenly, without warning, the gorilla reached for a rope and swung from his branch, crashing with an almighty bang onto the wall, right alongside Lilian, causing her to jump with a shriek into the air. His party piece, we are told. I have a sneaking suspicion that they all knew the exact spot where Lilian had to stand to appreciate the full effect of his antic. Perhaps he gets a commission of bananas from the local laundry? But Lilian had not finished yet: now I got my laugh after the pixie's egg cup episode, because as we watched the feeding of the ring-tailed lemurs, Chris Ryder gleefully turned to Lilian and said, 'In you go.'

Sensing the absolute horror in her eyes, I asked if she would like me to go in with her.

'No, you did your bit in the pottery, now it's my turn,' she said. So in she went, followed by the camera crew, who followed her every movement. Chris winked at me and whispered, 'Now follow her in,' and unbeknown to her, I stood right behind her, as, transfixed with fear, she proffered bits of food to these strange creatures with the sharp teeth. They were taking grapes from her hand when suddenly I put both of my hands on her shoulders. She told me afterwards that she thought she had a lemur on her back, which didn't do much to improve her confidence (aren't I rotten?).

'It's O.K., it's me, Darling,' I said. Maybe it was that moment that we fell in love with each other?

One of the cages we were shown had a sign which led us to believe it contained an Orang-utan, but all I could see was what appeared to be a small heap of sacks in a corner. Was that him? Apparently so, but he was not receiving guests that day.

Our hosts very kindly presented us each with a video of the zoo, a reminder of that happy event. We now had to leave, back to the hotel for lunch.

It was very pleasing to sit together in the limousine: we waved to people we passed, who gave us curious glances, no doubt wondering, 'Who are they?' It was the first time, but not to be the last, it so transpired, that we would travel in such comfort.

We were told that a candlelit dinner for two had been arranged for the evening, so we decided on a light lunch. Now I am very fond of mussels, but I wasn't prepared for the huge bowl which appeared in front of me. After a gallant attempt I managed to consume about a third of the contents, but to my chagrin I had to admit defeat over the rest.

Now was the time for us all to relax, and with our fellow travellers from London Weekend Television, we enjoyed a drink at the bar. We were pleased that a fellow guest, who, incidentally, had appeared on an earlier edition of *Blind Date*, took a photograph of us all, a copy of which holds a proud place in our lounge today.

Come the evening, we were shown to a table set in front of the dance floor and immediately opposite the pianist. What a magnificent meal, a bottle of champagne on ice, and excellent food. I think that I drank most of the champagne; Lilian, I found out, was not a lover of champagne or any wine for that matter, but was more partial to Tia Maria, but who's complaining? We ate and drank under the floodlights, by now becoming quite used to the camera so that it held no fear for us.

We danced alone on the floor, not knowing why the other diners were not joining in. Perhaps they felt that they might be intruding? The pianist smiled and gave us the thumbs-up sign as he played *When I Fall In Love*, so romantic, so perfect an evening. Isobel, Lilian's chaperone, and the camera crew disappeared from the scene and we were on our own, so we finished our meal and retired to the lounge for a Tia Maria and a Cognac to reflect on our day.

A lady and gentleman, fellow guests in the hotel, congratulated us as they passed through the lounge, and sent the waiter in with drinks with their compliments. We were still holding hands whilst sitting on the settee as our day came to an end, long after midnight.

The morning of the second day, Lilian was going for the *Bish Bash*, the term used for that part of the show where we expose our thoughts and feelings about each other, and which appears on the show one week later.

'Will you come back next week and tell us all about it?' Cilla asks.

I waited downstairs whilst Lilian was being interviewed, and here it is, in Lilian's own writing: -

Here goes, off to my *Bish Bash*: sounds ominous, doesn't it? But it really was a 'lorra, lorra' laughs and fun. It was so hilarious I almost collapsed on the floor with laughter. Every time I said something in answer to a question, I turned to Kevin Paice, the sound technician, and I would say, 'Was that alright, Kevin?'

His reply would be, 'No! Do it again.' The others couldn't stop laughing as I had to say it over and over again. Stupid me! I kept thinking I'd better say it differently this time. Midst all the laughter Kevin would pull an imaginary zip across his mouth, which only made matters worse, and it was laughter all the way. Finally I managed it without saying, 'Is that alright, Kevin?' We sat around discussing it, and Chris Ryder who was directing the interview, asked me what I thought of Cilla's hat that she wore at the first *Blind Date* wedding. My answer was, 'Horrible!'.

'No, seriously, Lilian, what did you think?' he repeated.

'It was horrible, and it made her look awful,' I replied.

'Guess what? We've just recorded this conversation and we're keeping it to blackmail you.'

By this time tears of laughter were streaming down my face. What a team, they were fabulous, every one of them. They all made a fuss of us both. Of course, they could see that we had fallen in love with each other, and thought we were great, that was the way we thought of them also, our thanks to them all for a super date.

Waiting downstairs, time went by and I was wondering what was happening up there? Then Lilian appeared, all smiles, and it was my turn. The interview was held in a pleasant room with a sea view, crammed with lights, cameras, sound equipment, and a chair for me. I was asked general questions, for instance what I thought of my date when I first saw her, how did we get on together? and points of interest that would appeal to the viewers about our short relationship.

Sometimes it was necessary for several *takes*, once or twice I made a false start and got lost, but I must say everybody was very patient. We had a lot of laughs, and eventually completed the job.

After lunch, Lilian and I packed our cases, and Isobel escorted us to St. Helier, leaving us there to do some shopping, and arranged to meet us later. Browsing around the shops together seemed to appeal to us both, as we strolled, still holding hands. We bought some small gifts to take home for relatives and friends, and one special gift I bought for Lilian, a butterfly brooch, which subsequently was lost, due I am sure to a rather insecure clasp. Sitting on a bench talking together I told Lilian that I had been thinking of taking a cruise on the P & O cruise liner Canberra to the Mediterranean (it had been my daughter Georgina's suggestion during my period of showing lack of interest that I take a cruise, and she had appeared one day with a whole armful of brochures for me to consider, which I did, and the one I mention had appealed to me). So when telling Lilian of my thoughts, I asked her if she would like to come with me. I didn't have to wait long for an answer, because she said there and then that she would.

Off to the airport, time to wave goodbye to Jersey as we boarded. Again we were sitting together in the forward seats, and the stewardess approached and said, 'Excuse me, if you two could tear yourselves apart, the Captain invites you, one at a time, to come to the flight deck.'

I didn't need to be asked twice, and gladly went forward and was belted in between and behind the Pilot and Co-Pilot. From where I sat I could see take-off, and watched on the monitor screen the outline of the coast and the positions of ships in the Channel. Then it was Lilian's turn, and we changed places. It really was a new experience for me, and for Lilian, who although in the WAAF during the war, as ground crew, had never been so near to the cockpit as on this occasion. Our thanks to the Pilot and Co-Pilot, hopefully you will read this book and remember.

Back in England now, and a taxi to the Russell Hotel. After breakfast I took Lilian to King's Cross, bade her goodbye and made my way to Paddington and home.

Arriving there, I was greeted with great anticipation of my news, and I had a lot to talk about. I was feeling on top of the world, I had had a wonderful date with a wonderful woman. I could not have asked for, nor expected, more. And there was still the anticipation of the other meeting in a few days time, when I would see her again. The time could not pass quickly enough for me, and I wondered how other contestants who had been on their dates felt when they returned after parting from their 'date' partners.

There must have been some lucky ones who felt the way I did. Some no doubt disappointed, some elated, and I'll warrant, some not really sure of their feelings.

Two total strangers brought together in romantic surroundings fosters the loving feelings, which could, if both felt the same way, lead into, if not marriage, but good friendship. Alas, as we see on some of the programmes, this does not appear always to be the case. However, I feel certain that many of the relationships so formed hold the participants in good staid for any future encounters they may have with the opposite sex. After all, without relationships of a loving nature, what future is there?

I must also bring in Lilian's own feelings at this stage, and the best way to put them is in her own words.

Leaving David, I felt a little sad, but there was the going back to sit on the settee next week, also we had arranged to telephone each other every night. David said to me, 'Don't worry, the time will soon pass and we will be together again.' He settled me on a seat in the train and stayed until the last moment. Once I'd settled down the excitement flooded over me and I wanted to tell all the other passengers that I had met a wonderful man. I didn't of course. On my arrival at Newcastle I rang Belle to make sure that she was home, so that I could go straight to her and give her my good news. After hugs and kisses and a cup of tea, plus a bite to eat, with something stronger we celebrated my happiness. Naturally I chatted a hundred to the dozen, then left by taxi for my flat at Grasmere House. Dot, my warden, saw the taxi arrive and came out to greet me, saying, 'Well, how did it go?'

'Absolutely fabulous!'

Then she said something strange, she said, 'There's a glow about you.'

'I met a wonderful man and we fell in love with each other!' I said.

Soon most of the residents knew about David, and were asking when were they going to meet him? I just laughed happily and said that it would be soon. When eventually they did meet him I believe most of them fell for him too, and I was not surprised.


Back to me, David, now, and when I read what she said, what could I say? We took turns to telephone each other every evening until it was time to return to London for our *On The Settee With Cilla* session.

Helped by Isobel's intricate timing of trains, we both arrived at the studio in the same taxi: there was no trying to keep us apart this time. Then up to our dressing rooms and make-up ready for our appearance. We were the last part of the evening's show, and listening to the result of the *Bish Bash*, Cilla was impressed by our apparent liking for each other (we were still holding hands). Lilian told Cilla that I had asked her to go on a cruise with me on the *Canberra*, to the Mediterranean. Cilla said, 'On the Canberra, for about a week then?'

'Twelve days,' I replied.

'Does this mean I've got to buy a new 'at?' asked Cilla.

Then Lilian perked up with, 'You're not coming in that other one.' Women!

Lilian said that she was coming with me to Devon the next day for a holiday, and to Cilla's question that if anything did happen, where would we live?

'Devon,' replied Lilian.

Whereupon Cilla wished the both of us a 'lorra, lorra luck for the future'.

# Chapter 4

## After the Date, and build-up to the Wedding.

Lilian came back with me to Devon, for a holiday, and stayed at my daughter's home, where I was living at the time. I had invited her so that she could meet my family, and I could show her how and where I lived. I believed that she would get to know me better if she shared my environment, and the beautiful countryside, a long way from the entrapment and the rigours of life in a heavily populated town. Not that I have any hang-ups about town life, I hasten to add. I had spent many years working in the heart of the City of London, and considered myself a part of that busy metropolis. I suppose many would liken the country life to be more or less on a perpetual holiday. Especially so, of course when, like Lilian and I, people have retired. There are drawbacks, as Lilian has found out: whereas the towns usually smell of petrol and diesel fumes, these are not so noticeable here, it's the animal farmyard smells that sometimes pervade the area. In plain words, an almighty stink! It invariably occurs at its worst when we have visitors, with the wind blowing in the wrong direction. But on the whole, Lilian has taken to it like a duck to water.

It had been on my mind to ask Lilian to be my wife; now I am not a true gambler, although I admit to buying lottery tickets, but to ask a woman whom I loved to marry me was a gamble that I believed to be heavily loaded in my favour. If she loved me as much, then her answer would most likely be 'yes'. If, on the other hand, ten years of living on her own had firmly entrenched her views then there was always the possibility of a firm 'no'. Particularly as I had learnt that, after the failure of her first marriage, she had vowed never to marry again.

So the possibility of a polite 'No, thank you,' or 'I'll think about it' could not be entirely eliminated. One of her dancing partners, whom she had known for several years, had asked Lilian to marry him five times. Five times! Now what were the odds? So the question was a gamble, and I took it.

One evening, while sitting in front of the log burner in the walk-in fireplace, I got down on one knee (not the wonky one) and asked Lilian if she would marry me. Beaming all over her face, she said, 'Yes, please.'

Had her answer been 'No, thank you' or 'No fear' or even 'not on your nelly' I have no idea what would have happened next, but I expect we would have remained firm friends, maybe still going on holidays together, who knows? But there is one thing I can add with certainty: you wouldn't be reading this book!

This book wouldn't be complete if I did not at this point say how pleased I was, and how lucky, my life had now taken on a new meaning.

We could have named this book *Yes Please*, but I'm sure that title has been used before, or was it *Please Sir*? But any title other than the one we have chosen would not have been so appropriate, in our opinion. After all, if Lilian had said 'Number One', or even 'Number Three, please', then of course I would not be sitting here fumbling with the myriad of keys on this word processor. Instead, I would most probably be having an interesting time watching the grass grow.

Talking about word processors, I am fortunate in that I have a good neighbour, Darren, who has been of great help when I have had problems with this machine, putting me right when I felt that perhaps it needed some more oil! However, he did assure me that it would have been easier if I had grown up with computers. Alas! I am one of those poor unfortunate beings for whom such equipment is beyond comprehension. I have a video machine, well, two between Lilian and I, one of which I believe is capable of being programmed for something on the TV a year from now. I don't know what's on next week until I buy the appropriate book or paper, and if any reader can tell me what's on twelve months from now I shall be pleased to hear from them.

After Lilian had agreed to marry me I told Georgina, who was in the next room. She came in, kissed Lilian and said, 'I'm not surprised, he's done nothing but talk about you since you first met.' There was a telephone call between us and Chris O'Dell of LWT. Chris asked how we were after the show, so Lilian told him of our engagement. We think that Chris was a little taken aback with this news because he said, 'Are you sure, Lilian, is David sure? I'm beginning to sound like your parents.' To this day I am convinced that the answer to his query about how we were feeling after the show was not quite the response he would be expecting after a somewhat routine conversation with two of his older contestants. We then telephoned Lilian's daughter Linda to inform her of our decision, and she said that she was pleased for her Mum.

We had decided to drive to Newcastle, but Linda suggested we meet her first. So, slight change of plan, a drive to Liverpool instead. It was late when we reached Liverpool, and we missed the turn-off we should have taken on the East Lancs' road to the Bell Tower Hotel and got lost, but eventually it was all sorted. I met Linda, husband Tony, granddaughter Clair and grandson Colin. I must say how nice it was for me to meet Lilian's family, and feel so warmly welcome. Secretly they must have thought that the *old girl* had gone off her rocker. I would have liked to have been a fly on the wall to hear what they said when we had gone. They gave us our first engagement present, a silver photo frame.

The next day was Sunday, a trip to the Albert Dock complex was decided upon, a stroll among the many small shops and a visit to the coffee shop. Floating on the water was the model of the British Isles that Fred the weather man jumps about on and I thought that it looked a lot larger when seen on the TV screen.

It was time to continue our travels, so off we drove to Newcastle-on-Tyne to Lilian's home in Walker. It's a lovely little flat and Lilian, the generous hearted lady that she is, insisted that the bedroom would be mine, and she would sleep on the settee in the lounge. Now you may consider that a gentleman would insist on the lady having the better accommodation, but I had begun to realise that, small though she may be, she was a very strong willed and incidentally clever woman. Anyway, she is shorter in height than I and fitted better on the couch.

I met Lilian's fellow residents and friends, most of whom congratulated us when we told them the news, and there began a steady stream of rings on the door bell and cards in the letter box.

It was off to the city centre, with a very special objective in mind: Samuel's the Jewellers. Peering in the window, we admired a diamond cluster ring, so decided to pop in and try it on Lilian's finger. All happy, we left the shop with the little box holding Lilian's new engagement ring. One more stage had been reached in the process of a typical man and woman relationship. Everything was now gathering momentum.

Back at the flat all the ladies wanted to see her ring which had looked so attractive in the shop window, and which looked even better when worn on her finger. Lilian had whispered to the young assistant who served us about the circumstances of our engagement, and the assistant said she would watch the show when it came on the air.

The next ring was the telephone, Thelma McGough, Producer of *Blind Date*, with a request that we meet for lunch in London on the eighth of November. A request to which we were both happy to agree.

I drove home to Devon after kissing Lilian goodbye for the present, I was happy in the knowledge that we would be meeting again in a few day's time in London. Parting and seeing each other again had become for us both a way of life, and we could put up with this in the interim period. We must have each covered many hundreds of rail miles during this time. But at least we had an ultimate goal to which we could look forward with great anticipation.

A carefully planned timing schedule had been arranged for us on the eighth, I would be met at Paddington station by taxi, then proceed to Kings Cross station to pick up Lilian, so that we would both arrive at the studio together. My train was late in arriving, I was getting edgy, hurrying down the platform where I was relieved to see my name on the taxi driver's board. No way can one make a quick dash through the heart of London by road, especially during the peak hours. My driver was excellent, and made use of his skill in avoiding the worst of the congested areas. I jumped out of the taxi and fairly ran into the station, with the driver in hot pursuit.

And there was Lilian, walking down the platform from the train which had just arrived. Phew! I must admit that I had been worried, what would she have done if we hadn't been there to meet her as arranged? She wasn't a native of London. As it turned out my fears had been groundless, I know now that she would have assessed the situation quite calmly and waited a reasonable time before making her way by taxi to the destination. Silly me! Panic over, we arrived and were introduced to the Director, Kevin Roast, and together with Thelma McGough and Zoe McIntyre we departed for the National Theatre Restaurant for lunch.

The object of the meeting was to discuss our forthcoming marriage, and the impact that this would have on the Press, once they knew of the engagement. Zoe, Press Officer, was assigned to assist us in the matter of press coverage. Lilian showed them her new ring, and they all congratulated us.

On reflection back to that meeting, I can understand how concerned they had been regarding the publicity, after all, it had only happened once before in the history of the show, and it was out of the blue. Wham! A wedding! Don't get me wrong, they may have been surprised, but they were very happy for us. We feel sure that our eventual wedding did a little bit to enhance the popularity of the programme.

We never had any reason to criticise the help of LWT in the arrangements. We were always treated with great respect, and they made us feel like royalty.

Rooms had been booked for us at the Rembrandt Hotel where we received a phone call, and were told that we would be having an exclusive interview with *The Sun* newspaper the following morning.

Waiting in the hotel foyer we noticed a man walking about carrying a huge bouquet of flowers.

'I wonder if they are for you?' I said to Lilian. Sure enough, a few moments later Zöe walked in and came straight to us, whereupon the gentleman with the bouquet came over too, introduced himself and presented Lilian with the flowers. After the interview the photographer drove us into Hyde Park, taking lots of pictures, some of us kicking up the leaves, some with me holding Lilian, somewhat precariously I might add. Was she heavy, or was I so weak? It was the latter, I'm pleased to add.

The article, together with the picture of me lifting Lilian, came out in the November the eleventh edition. Now the whole country knew that we were to be married. It would be the second marriage in the *Blind Date* ten year history.

I went with Lilian to Kings Cross to see her off to Newcastle before returning to Devon.

It was Lilian's intention to pack or dispose of a lot of her possessions, as we had decided that our future together would be in Devon. There were many arrangements to make and Lilian was due to take part in a fashion show being put on by the Wallsend branch of the British Heart Foundation, which I will tell you about later.

Whilst she was back in her Newcastle home Lilian paid a visit to the well known store, Fenwicks, to choose her Bridal outfit. She chose a Frank Usher cream two piece suit, which I was not to see until our wedding day. Her size not being in stock, a phone call to the Bond Street branch confirmed that a size ten was available and would be dispatched right away. Matching cream shoes were also on her agenda. At this time the headdress was also purchased, plus matching bouquet, both in cream silk flowers adorned with pearls and crystals. Reflecting back to the wedding day, I cannot help but think what a great choice she had made. She was to me a perfect picture of happiness.

Both of us were receiving telephone calls from newspapers, periodicals and radio stations, all of which we referred back to LWT press office as a safeguard for them and for us. This arrangement worked very well. At this point, I would like to say that we have always been treated with respect by the press.

We have had a few saucy headlines, for example:-

**Blind Date Oldies Can't Wait For Bedded Bliss** (*News of the World*, Jan 16th 1994)
**Blind Date Oldies Set Up Love Nest** (*The People*, Jan 16th 1994)
**I Missed Wedding Night Nookie, I Fell Asleep In The Bath** (*The Sun*, Feb. 12th 1994)
**'Blind Date Kissogram Gran, 71, Weds TV Fella'** (The Sun Oct llth 1993)

All in good fun, and we have no complaints. The majority of news items about us were very complimentary. I have four scrap books filled with press cuttings and it looks as though I may need more. I can only recall one report that criticised our intended marriage. This article in a northern newspaper, written by a lady critic wished us happiness, but confessed her disappointment when she learnt of our ages, seventy and seventy one. She hoped that when people got to that age they should have grown out of the agonies of falling in love. She also went on to say that she would have thought Lilian would be happy with a nice new hot water bottle, a knitting pattern, and something good on the television. Then she concluded that maybe television watching isn't the harmless activity you'd think. After all, if Lilian hadn't watched *Blind Date* she wouldn't be planning another wedding.

Oh well, you can't please everybody, can you?

Later, I wrote what I consider to be quite a nice letter to the lady concerned, and asked if she watched our wedding on the television, with of course her hot water bottle and her knitting. Sad to say, my letter was ignored and didn't appear in the press. That's life.

However, if by some strange quirk of fate that lady is reading this book, don't drop a stitch when you realise it's you I'm writing about. I hope you feel honoured when so much about you is appearing in my book. No hard feelings, and good luck to you.

While we are on the subject of knitting, I will tell you that Lilian does a great deal of knitting, especially while travelling in the car as a passenger. She knits these little jumpers for Save the Children and for the Oxfam shop in Tiverton. Since she has become my wife, in nine months she has knitted one hundred and ten. If I remember, when I reach the end of the last chapter, I will try to give you the latest score.

Come the fourth of December the *Blind Date* show was on the TV. I watched it on my own, and positively cringed when I saw myself get up on my feet and sing *Any Old Iron*. But I had done it, and that was that.

Lilian watched the show later when I came up before Christmas, as she wanted us to watch it together and not on her own, so she had taped it on her video for that purpose. When we watched it we were both emotional, it looked good, Lilian was thrilled how well it went. Then the 'On the settee' was on the box, and it was good to watch it straight after the show recording. This was how Lilian had planned it, she fancied us both seeing the two together. We thought it was great, sitting there, holding hands, as usual, reliving every detail together.

The show apparently had quite a big viewing, particularly as many had seen the press and wondered what had happened to create such furore. One of the results from the broadcast was the surprising increase in our mail. We were having so many letters, all of them wishing us happiness, saying how they had enjoyed the show, and many speaking of their own experiences, some happy, some sad. All wrote saying that Lilian had picked the right one for her, quite a few said that they had jumped up and down shouting 'Pick Number Two'. What lovely letters. Indeed we now have a regular correspondence with a number of those original writers. This is Lilian's domain, she is the personal letter correspondent. I mostly deal with the rest. It has taken Lilian just over a year to answer every one of those letters herself. Quite a lot of the mail came via the television studios and was forwarded on, some via the local post office, others such as 'The romantic couple, Devon'. What a really marvellous postal system we have, when you consider the addresses they had to go on. It was becoming quite usual to be stopped in the street and congratulated,

Taxi drivers were hooting as they passed, and, amazingly enough, it still goes on. We are quite used to the winding down of car windows and the passengers calling, 'The best of luck to you both'. What a fantastic reception we were now experiencing. One favourite question is, 'How's our Cilla?

It had been agreed between Lilian and I that I would travel by train to Newcastle on Saturday the eleventh of December, the day on which the *Blind Date* show would include our 'on the couch' session with Cilla. However, several days before this, our only contact being by telephone, I became restless.

'What are you doing here?' asked Georgina.

I needed no second bidding: the next day I was off to see my dear Lilian, who met me at Central station, and we were back together again. We watched the show on television, and immediately after, left the flat and waited at the bus stop around the corner. Three youngsters approached us and one said, 'You are the two who have just been on the television, on *Blind Date*, aren't you? How did you get here from London so quick? Have you just come back from your date?' The magic of television.

Two days later we had put on a farewell party at Grasmere House, with an open invitation for all residents, plus Lilian's relatives and friends including those from the Heart Foundation where she had worked. At the time we felt that it would be impractical for most of them to attend the wedding in

Devon, due to the cost involved for the individuals, the problem of limited accommodation around the village, and the transport difficulties. There was also the fact that the reception had to be limited in number due to the seating capacity. The residents kindly presented us with a wedding present of a carriage clock, which sits on the top of our television today.

The following day we attended the fashion show put on by the Wallsend branch of the Heart Foundation. Lilian took part with the others, and it was great, a very enjoyable evening. It concluded with Lilian and I appearing on the catwalk wearing evening togs, announced as their local celebrities, to the recorded music of *Love Changes Everything*, a nice touch!

Lilian had been very busy packing up her home prior to leaving Newcastle. Quite a lot of her furniture and personal trinkets she gave away, being the generous person that she was. The rest she arranged to be picked up and delivered by van to Devon.

Lilian's suit had to be picked up from Fenwicks, so, with friend Belle, off we went to town. I was dumped in the restaurant, where I engaged in conversation with two charming ladies who spotted me as having been on television. Lilian and Belle had been to the French salon, and returned with a big bag which I was told not even to peek into. Shame! Now it so happened that we passed through the lingerie department, where we stopped to admire some pure silk underwear in delightful shades of green. At this point Lilian had been asked to show her ring, and very soon staff and customers were all gathering around, and we seemed to be attracting a lot of attention.

I asked Lilian if she would like to have the silk garments, but she declined saying that they were too expensive. Great stuff, this, she was keeping an eye on my spending. However, Belle, who had been surveying the whole scene with interest, said to the assistant, 'She'll have three pairs.'

Whereupon the assistant turned to Lilian and said, 'Which colours would madam like?'

Lilian's reaction was to look terrified, and replied, 'Oh! Oh! No thank you!'

Our friendly assistant then disappeared into the stockroom and came out holding the largest pair of bloomers I had ever seen, saying, 'Would madam prefer a pair of these?'

We all collapsed into fits of laughter, the whole department seemed to be in uproar. This incident, as it happened, was to appear later on the front page of their store magazine, with our picture. Belle, many years younger than Lilian said, 'I'm the bride's mother, and I haven't got anything yet.'

I took the opportunity of purchasing Lilian's Christmas present whilst I was there. What was it? I'm not telling. Phew, what a day that was, I must say that we thoroughly enjoyed every minute of it.

A telephone call from London requested that we attend a photo-call with Cilla. As we had already purchased our train tickets it was necessary for us to change them for break of journey. This we did on our next visit to town, and presented no problem. Another visit to Samuel's was necessary for us to buy our wedding rings, a neat little diamond one for the lady and a plain gold band which I fancied, for myself. Here was the opportunity to select the Bridesmaids' presents, and it was a very nice touch when the shop manager gave Lilian a spray of flowers with the compliments of the staff. Lilian then went off to the Gateshead Metro Centre in a search of a dress for her Spanish Bridesmaid. The search proved to be fruitful.

The next morning we departed, and Lilian's friends Dot, Margaret, and Emma were there to wave us goodbye.

For the photo-call we were required to dress in full wedding outfits, Lilian in a cream suit and hat, me in top hat and tails. The shoes for Lilian to wear did not fit, but fortunately Lilian had with her the shoes she had just purchased for her wedding outfit, so problem solved. After shots of us together were taken we changed into less formal outfits. Cilla had now arrived with her husband Bobby, and it was the first time we had met the Great Lady and her husband together, and it was for us a memorable occasion. Cilla, Lilian and I had some great pictures taken, which were to appear later in a number of publications.

We completed our journey to Devon, and awaited the arrival of the van bringing Lilian's belongings. Now you may think that this would not be a very exciting episode to include in this book, but you would be mistaken. It rained heavily all day, and due to some excavation work on the hillside, outside the farmhouse door was thick mud. Therefore I kept a lookout for the van's arrival to limit its approach. Its arrival had been expected late afternoon, but it was near 10.00 pm when it appeared. I dashed out to halt its progress, but was too late, the front wheels sank in the mud up to the axles. The driver, poor fellow, jumped out of the cab, right up to his knees in the morass, pitched forward and fell full length. All this in total darkness and pouring rain. The rest of this episode I could only describe as mud, mud, and more mud. It was well after midnight when all Lilian's bits and pieces, including her three piece suite had been off-loaded, by which time we were all soaking wet, muddy and, dare I say it, slightly, but only slightly, peeved! It took the ancient tractor and all available hands eventually to get the vehicle back onto solid ground. Lilian, what did I do to deserve all this?

Discussions took place with LWT regarding the date for the wedding, resulting in a mutually agreed February the fifth 1994, which date gave us time to prepare and arrange all the details.

The Registry Office at Tiverton was contacted and confirmed the date as acceptable. The Reverend Tony Grosse of St. Mary's Church, Hemyock, also accepted that date for the Blessing. A strict timetable was later prepared to ensure the smooth running of the whole procedure.

Lilian and I had initially decided that the reception would be held at a local Inn, but as the arrangements proceeded, and the number of guests to be invited increased, doubts as to the capacity at that venue arose, particularly as space for the cameras and associated gear was necessary in the building. Chris O'Dell and ourselves visited the Inn and another possible venue, Burnworthy Manor, at Churchstanton, owned by Liz and Rupert Phillips. The latter proved to be the more suitable, a silk-lined marquee would be erected in the grounds, and the manor house rooms would be made available to the guests. It was agreed that eighty guests could be accommodated for the reception and meal. We will always be grateful for the organising assistance we received from Chris and his team. Without their help none of this would have been achieved, or would have progressed so smoothly.

All the invitations were duly despatched and the replies awaited. At this stage concern was raised about the seating capacity of both the Registry Office and the Church. Passes were therefore prepared and sent to guests, to ensure priority at both venues.

Rhona Gillmore, Beauty Consultant, offered to give Lilian complimentary facial treatment before the wedding, which she was pleased to accept.

Susan McCulloch, opera singer of fame, contacted LWT and offered to sing at the Church Blessing, which we accepted with gratitude.

There was yet another surprise to come. Peter Reckless, of the Birmingham Jewellery quarter, did contact LWT with the offer of making our wedding rings for us, but as we had already purchased them, it was suggested that he make an Eternity ring for Lilian. This necessitated dispatching to him her wedding ring, so that he could make the eternity ring to match, which he did, and a fine ring it was.

Accompanied by Zöe, LWT Press officer, we had an appointment with a *News of the World* journalist. Lilian did an exclusive interview, and it appeared the following Sunday. I was pleased when I read it, Lilian had done a first class job, and the following day Thelma rang from London to congratulate her.

Queen's College, Taunton, offered to send their pupil string quartet to the Church to play whilst the guests were assembling. We had the Order of Service printed locally, and featured the string quartet, Susan McCulloch, who would be singing *One Hand, One Heart* from the musical *West Side Story* and *Love Changes Everything* from *Aspects of Love*.

We did our utmost to book accommodation for those requiring it, and personally visited the places before advising the guests of their arrangements, to ensure satisfaction.

Jill Redmond of the Country Wedding Co. contacted us, offering complimentary wedding cars for the occasion, an offer which we gratefully accepted, and I can tell you that riding in those immaculate white cars on the day was really quite an experience. Jill produced a strict schedule for the timing of each run, and I understood that each journey was carefully rehearsed before the big day was due to arrive.

*Good Morning TV* invited us to London to appear on the morning show with Lorraine Kelly, to talk about the forthcoming wedding. This we accepted, duly arrived and waited in the *Green room*, whereupon Mr Motivator popped in and said 'Hello'. We were welcomed by Lorraine to the show, who commented that it was nice to see two people who had come together through the *Blind Date* show. She said that in a lot of cases they did not get on with each other, but that 'Spectacularly' (Lorraine's own words) they didn't like each other. We had to agree that appeared to be the case. After discussing our wedding plans, Lorraine congratulated us both on the forthcoming event, and she presented Lilian with a large bouquet of flowers, and for me a bottle of champagne. Great!

You may consider that we had a fairly busy time, but I can assure all readers that it had only just started. By now the telephone was continually ringing, and we didn't know what to expect next.

We didn't have long to wait, a call from *This Morning* in Liverpool inviting us to appear on the Richard and Judy show. We were off again by train to Liverpool. I reckon that British Rail made a packet out of our marriage, I had never made so many long distance train journeys in such a short space of time, in my life. Which reminds me of a memorable train journey I made during the war: I was at a transit camp in Cornwall, and drafted to join a ship in Rothesay. I had to change trains, it was either Paddington or Crewe, I'm not sure which, but the gentleman who made out my itinerary had only allowed me two minutes to get from one platform to the other, with me carrying all my kit! Well, I missed the connection, didn't I? So I missed the last ferry along the Clyde, the journey took me two days. When I presented myself on board and reported to the Skipper, he said, 'You will take fourteen days foreign service leave, starting right away,' so I had to travel practically all the way back.

But that has nothing to do with the Richard and Judy show, I'm glad to say, because this was going to be a most pleasurable experience. We were met and driven to the Redbourn Hotel at Woolton for the night. Come the morning, we were picked up by car and arrived at the Albert Dock studios. Lilian's daughter and friend met us at the studio and were accommodated in the visitors' lounge, where they could view the show on the television monitor screen.

We learnt afterwards that Linda and friend met Fred the weatherman, and had a good laugh together, and a photograph taken with him. Oh yes?!

Richard and Judy introduced us with the *Blind Date* theme, depicting our meeting on the show. Andrew Collinge, hairdresser of the year, Lesley Ebbetts, fashion expert, and Rhona Gillmore, Lilian's makeover consultant, were all present on the set. Judy said that she was impressed with Lilian on the *Blind Date* show, and asked her if she worked out, Lilian said that she did not. Richard also asked me the same question, Did I work out? and my answer was the same.

Rhona said that she had been doing Acupuncture points on Lilian's face preparatory to the wedding, also that Lilian was a 'warm season'. Andrew did a hair and beard trim on myself whilst we were on the set. He also remarked that Lilian was quite adept at putting up her own hair. Lesley Ebbetts stated that I had been having a few problems with my clothing for the wedding occasion, which she was helping me to sort out.

After a break, we both returned to the set, accompanied by a round of applause. Lilian was now wearing a blue 'Eastex' suit, costed by Lesley at about one hundred and fifty pounds. Her hair had been re-styled by Andrew, which she turned to show a pearl clasp set in the back, as on the day Lilian would not be wearing a hat.

Lesley said that she had had a slight problem with me, in that I had stated a preference for a blue suit, but that she had come up with a smart blue-grey double breasted suit, which I was wearing. Together with a fancy silk waistcoat and a pink silk tie, this made up my outfit. We were complimented on our appearance, and Lesley told us that they would be giving us these outfits.

Judy told us that we now would be meeting Joan Collins, and when she came on the set she said that she thought we looked wonderful, and that she loved Lilian's hair. Wasn't that nice of her? She congratulated us on finding love together, and said that she herself was a *Blind Date* fan.

Then Judy said to Lilian, 'David is staying at your home?'

To which Lilian replied, 'No, I'm staying in David's home, and I'm sleeping on the sofa.'

So Joan said, 'Well, you haven't got to know each other yet.'

Joan and I had a little chat together, then it was a glass of champagne all round to toast our forthcoming wedding. What a memorable and exciting day that was.

About this time, Cilla appeared in *The Sun* newspaper, in a *New 'at* phone-in competition, to help her decide which of seven hats we, the public, would most like to see her wearing at the wedding. We naturally registered our own vote on this one.

Jane Asher phoned to say that *TV Weekly* would like to give us a wedding cake, and that she, Jane, would be making it, and would we come to her Chelsea cake shop to discuss the design? Well, this was another kindness which we gratefully accepted. So off we went to town again, this time to meet Jane and marvel at the enormous range of different styles of cake that can be made. We settled for a three tier hexagon design, each with the *Blind Date* logo and *DL* on alternate facets. The two pigs on the top were Lilian's suggestion; she told Jane that I had a collection of pottery pig miniatures in my home.

Shortly after our visit we were invited back to Chelsea for the presentation of the finished cake, beautifully made by Jane. Debbie Greenwood presented it to us on behalf of *TV Weekly*. What generosity we were experiencing. Mike Vaughan, photographer, took some shots of Jane, the cake, and us. Another great day for us.

*GMTV* telephoned to suggest that we may like to go on a 'shopping spree' with them, followed by an appearance on the television show with Eamonn Holmes and Lorraine Kelly. This time it was to Dickins and Jones of Regent Street, where we arrived complete with our hostess and a camera crew.

We were escorted to the 'Personal Shopping Suite' situated in the ladies wear department, where there were trained staff ready to assist ladies in their selection of suitable apparel. A really great idea, and one which suited me down to the ground. Now this was the way for a man to shop, here I was, sat in a comfortable chair, with a coffee in my hand, whilst Lilian, aided by two cheerful ladies, was adorned in various suits, each time emerging from a cubicle for my inspection and comments. I would say quite truthfully that she looked great in all of them. Eventually, however, the particular outfit that we all admired had to be her final choice. It was a lime green short jacket with navy trousers. I liked it very much, and Lilian wore it whilst on the honeymoon. It was then my turn to visit the gentlemen's department, and after trying on suits of all shades, I chose a grey single breasted suit, which I was to wear during the wedding ceremony. Accompanied by the camera crew we then visited the bridal department, and enjoyed being photographed among the wedding models. The television show which we were to be on the following day had to be rearranged, we were told, so we did not meet Eamonn and Lorraine as planned. We were disappointed, of course, but these things happen.

It was now towards the end of January, and getting close to the day of the wedding. Much still had to be done, but everything was in hand, and the arrangements were flowing smoothly. Local and county newspapers were on the phone asking for permission for interviews and photographs, including calls from BBC Somerset Sound and Radio Devon.

Georgina and her friends took Lilian out for a 'Hen night' to a Chinese restaurant while I baby-sat with my grandchildren. Surprisingly enough, Lilian arrived home perfectly sober, but then her normal intake of alcoholic beverage never exceeded one glass. I thought she might have thrown caution to the wind as she was about to lose her single status, which she had enjoyed for so long.

You will read further in this book of my 'stag night', don't expect too much, the episode didn't go down as dramatically as it was probably expected to do, but nevertheless it was memorable, and had an unexpected conclusion.

We had been concerned about the white cars which would be carrying Lilian, myself, best man, bridesmaids and relatives from home to the Registry Office and the Church. They would have to negotiate the narrow country road leading to the farm. The endless days of continuous rain, coupled with the mud from the fields, conveyed by the tractors, had turned the road into a squelchy morass. I had visions of stopping en route to go through a car wash, and that was not advisable, especially for the open top cars. But then, out of the blue, about three days before the wedding, a road sweeping machine appeared and swept the whole length of the road. I've never found out to this day whether it was coincidental or that it was arranged by some kind person who was aware of the situation.

Chris and Annetta from LWT arrived to discuss the final arrangements for the big day. Also some of the camera crew came to discuss the requirements for the fixing of suitable lighting in the kitchen.

John Gorman and Thelma McGough arrived to fit Lilian with a personal microphone and battery pack, which they had specially prepared, covered in cream material so that it would not show through her suit. It was strapped around her waist, with the pack at the back, and arranged so that the cowl of the dress jacket covered it perfectly. Then the microphone was tucked inside the jacket, resulting in the whole thing being completely unnoticeable. We each had a detailed programme of events, there would be no slip-ups.

Friday the fourth of February, we arrived at St Mary's church in the morning for a rehearsal with the Reverend Tony. Goodness! I never expected this. The church was crowded with technicians with cables and lights everywhere. Ladies were arranging the flowers in pedestals and on the ends of the pews, right down the centre of the church. These flowers were a gift from Interflora and LWT, they were really lovely.

The Reverend Tony Grosse was instructing Lilian and I as to our positions and procedure for the Blessing, while Kevin Paice, sound technician, complete with his microphone (which I likened to a dead rabbit on a stick), hovered alongside, making faces and grinning at Lilian the while, causing my lady to go into fits of laughter. Annetta said, 'Don't worry, Lilian, we'll put a bag over his head tomorrow.'

As it turned out, a compromise was evidently reached, because they stuck Kevin behind a pillar, poor lad! Cilla had already arrived, all happy and smiling, and with her producer from the show, Thelma, they were discussing no doubt the arrangements for the next day. Everybody was so happy and cheerful, I knew at the time that it would be a very happy and colourful event, and I was proved right.

We had asked Lilian's brother Raymond and his friend Stephen and my son-in-law David if they would act as the ushers, which they both agreed to do, involving the checking of the passes at both Registry Office and the church, plus the distribution of the Orders of Service.

That evening, friends and relatives had arrived, some of whom were accommodated in the farmhouse. The house was packed. Lilian and I had to drive into Taunton to pick up friends Belle and Jim from Geordieland. We brought them back for a meal which Lilian had prepared, though I don't think Lilian and I ate very much: it's not easy with a telephone in one hand, which we passed to each other.

It was mainly news reporters and local radio stations, all wishing us to answer their questions over the phone. Lilian had only just taken the meal from the oven when this had all started. We had to leave them, Belle and

Jim that is, to help themselves. I believe we ended up with a chicken leg and a couple of cold potatoes, but we didn't care, excitement for us both was building up to a fever pitch.

Now, there was one more thing which had been arranged but not so far discussed. You're right, it was my stag night. It was only a short walk to the pub in the village, the Catherine Wheel, and come the evening, quite a few of the men had drifted in that direction. I said that I would follow, but had a couple of commitments to keep before so doing. One was to drive Lilian and her two friends to their accommodation in the next village, and the other, a last minute request by Lilian that I take her going-away outfit to the Burnworthy Manor where the reception was being held. So far, so good, but Lilian insisted on stopping at the pub to see if her brother Raymond had arrived. She went in on her own, whereupon the men said, 'What are you doing here?'

'David couldn't make it, so I've come instead.'

This caused a great deal of laughter among the men, most of whom by this time had consumed a fairly large quantity of the local brew, and were in an extremely jolly and happy mood. Whose wedding was this, anyway?

She then went up to Raymond and kissed him, and Raymond, with a look of surprise on his face, said, 'Who's this lady?'

Now Raymond is a great character, I had discovered, well known for his ready wit, a coach driver by trade, well thought of by his colleagues, and by those lucky enough to have travelled with him in his coach, both across the country and abroad, and he never missed an opportunity.

She dived out of the door into the car.

I hadn't reckoned how long it would take me, and how late it was by the time I got back to the pub after delivering Lilian's apparel, suffice it to say as I walked in the door the landlord was calling 'time'. Judging by their lack of amazement when I appeared, they had consumed sufficient quantities of ale to be past caring whether I turned up or not. I just had time for a quick glass of tonic water, then drove those who lacked the capability of walking up the road home. That was my stag night, and I thoroughly enjoyed it. Contrary to muttered suggestions previous to that night, I didn't end up stark naked tied to the handle of the village pump! I was stone cold sober, and enjoyed a good night's sleep.

# Chapter 5

## The Wedding

*Oh! what a beautiful morning*
*Oh! what a beautiful day,*
*I have a wonderful feeling*
*It's gonna be a wonderful wedding day.*

**Lilian**
Well, I just couldn't believe the wonderful sunshine, as it had poured with rain all week. Each day David had consoled me by saying the sun will shine on Saturday, and he was right. I had stayed the night at Thorn Cottage, with friends Belle and Jim, where I was very comfortable, got up early, had a bath and enjoyed a nice breakfast. My friends and I were collected by son-in-law Tony, and taken to the Travel Lodge, where a room had been put at my disposal for use when dressing and having my hair prepared in anticipation of the forthcoming event. My daughter Linda with family and friends had stayed at the same

lodge for two days, and brought with them their own hairdresser Ian from Liverpool to see to my mop. Ian styled my hair with a lovely French pleat, in which the headdress fitted nicely. Then came the camera and sound crew, everybody all go, but it was very enjoyable. Then came Rhona who was going to attempt to make me beautiful with her little pots of magic.

Whilst all this was going on, Linda came in to present me with a heart-shaped cushion, which she had embroidered in cross-stitch with 'Love to Lilian and David 5-2-94.' I was quite touched by this gesture. Another knock at the door, this time a young girl presented me with a magnificent bouquet of fresh flowers, made by Judith Goss and with the compliments of Interflora. Suddenly a voice came over the radio, wishing Lilian Morris and David Fensom a happy wedding day, and then playing a record of an old favourite of mine, Matt Monro's *Portrait Of My Love*. I made a little speech in which I thanked Cilla, because without her none of this would have happened.

Everyone had left and I was all alone. I stepped into my wedding outfit and took one last look in the mirror. Not bad! It was then off to Linda's room - she was more than pleased with what she saw, and Clair said, 'Oh! Grandma, you look gorgeous!'

The Travel Lodge staff were waiting in the foyer with their cameras at the ready. Grandson Colin, whom I had appointed to give me away, arrived looking very smart and handsome and I felt very proud as we stepped into the open topped white Beauford convertible which had now arrived to take us to the Registry Office. The weather was sunny, but with a cold wind, not surprising because it was February, but I was too excited to worry about feeling cold.

When the car entered Tiverton, I was so surprised to see thousands of people lining the pavements, in shop doorways and hanging out of upstairs windows, all waving and cheering. I must say that I felt as if I were Royalty as I waved back, wiping my eyes and saying to Colin that the wind had caught my eye. He just gave me a funny look and said, 'Oh yes, Grandma?'

I had composed myself by the time we had arrived at the Registry Office. The crowds outside the office were terrific, I just wished that I could have personally thanked everybody with a handshake. I was later told that some of them had waited four hours to see Cilla and us. I stood in the entrance and gave some more waves before walking inside and up the stairs, where friends and relatives were waiting to greet me. David's Best Man, Paul's brother Bill was there with his camcorder, when I reached the top of the stairs he called out to me to look his way, so that he could get some stills of me.

David was waiting for me with a hug and a kiss.

Well, that's my true version of the wedding so far, so it's over to him again.

## David

As Lilian has already said, it had been a week of continual rain, so when I woke up to see that the sun was shining, I knew that it would be a perfect day.

And a perfect day it transpired to be. After doing the usual things when one wakes up, bathing, shaving and eating, I was in the process of dressing, and entered the farmhouse kitchen, which I expected to see in its normal spick and span state, to see that it had been cleared of table and chairs, the centre pendant lights had been removed, and the room was bristling with Producer, technicians, cameras, floodlights and the inevitable wiring. Chris was busy preparing me for a brief interview on the camera, when the radio announcer wished us good luck for our wedding, and I heard the same broadcast of *Portrait Of My Love* by Matt Monro, that Lilian had simultaneously listened to. Then I said a few words about my feelings on what lay ahead. I can remember saying that when I applied for *Blind Date*, I had no idea what lay ahead: the publicity, the cameras, and that I was very proud and honoured to be part of it.

At about 11.00 am, a white Jaguar arrived to take Paul, my Best Man and myself to the Registry Office. As the car approached I noticed the barriers along each side of the road, with the police in attendance. My immediate thoughts were that the road was up, and it might be difficult to get close to the entrance. It then dawned on me that it might be due to the wedding, and this was confirmed when the Registry Office came into sight. Each side of the road was crammed with people. It had been estimated, I later learned, that over two thousand had lined the street. What a fantastic reception. Two of the bridesmaids arrived soon after, the other three were not present at the Registry Office, but appeared later at the Church ceremony.

Shortly after, Cilla and Bobby arrived, which evoked massive cheering from the assembled crowds, many of whom had waited a long time to see Cilla and of course, her new 'at.

Cilla waved to the crowds, more cheering.

There were now just two more to arrive, who were they?

Yes, of course it was Lilian with Colin. As I was inside the building I had to view these arrivals later on the television, and I must say that in my opinion the people who had waited all that time got their reward. I know I got mine when Lilian walked into the room and stood beside me. She was a real picture of beauty, I felt so proud to be the one who was going to become her husband. If her mother had been alive and could have seen her then, she would have been proud of her daughter. Before the ceremony commenced, both of us were being briefed in the back room by the Registrar, and, noticing that Lilian had a slight cough, due no doubt to dryness of the throat caused by the excitement, she gave Lilian a cough lozenge, and I had one also, which we immediately popped into our mouths. A few seconds later we were ushered into the official chamber, to a welcome with all the assembled standing and clapping. Do you know, I have never had such applause since the day I took part in a boat race at a holiday camp in the late 40's, when at the 'off', I took one mighty pull at the oars, they came out of the rowlocks and I did a lovely back somersault into the stern of the boat. The clapping rang in my ears for years after. To get back to those cough lozenges, did you know that we went through the whole of the ceremony sucking those lozenges, as we didn't like to be seen taking them out?

In a particular part of the ceremony, the giving of the rings, I had to repeat after the Registrar 'I give you this ring as a token of our marriage, and I call upon these persons here present, to witness that I, David Fensom, do take thee, Lilian Morris, to be my lawful wedded wife.' I don't know if anybody else noticed, but Lilian told me later that I missed out the words 'to witness'. Bad boy! Slap his hand!

After we had signed the register we were given a decorated wooden spoon from a well wisher, beautifully made with lace and diamante. Bobby asked if they were real. We were also given at that time a letter offering us a fishing weekend at Eggesford, with the compliments of Mid Devon Council, for what we had done for Tiverton. Kindness certainly surrounded us. After the handshakes and the photographs, Lilian and I opened and leaned out of the window to wave to the accumulated people outside, some of whom shouted 'Kiss her!' This was another very moving moment, there were so many happy smiling faces, we wanted to thank each and every one of them. One chap was perched somewhat precariously high up on some scaffolding immediately opposite the window. We gave him a special wave on his own for his achievement and resourcefulness. I hope he got down safely.

Now came the moment I believe everybody had waited for: Cilla, Lilian and I together in the doorway. I'll bet there were more cameras out than when the giant Pandas came out to take a bow at the zoo. Joking aside, however, it was another of those great moments, for, come to think of it there had been, and were to come, so many great moments: perhaps this book will help you, the reader, to share them with us.

As we left Tiverton it was a great scene, everybody waving, many wanting to shake our hands. After climbing into the white Beauford, with the hood down we drove through the cheering crowds to Hemyock. A quick visit to the farmhouse to re-form, then Paul and I were taken to St. Mary's Church, with the five Bridesmaids following in the next car.

The Ushers, David, Raymond and Steve had a busy time checking the passes of everyone arriving, issuing the Orders of Service, and thoroughly enjoying themselves in the meantime. It was fortunate for me that they did not ask to see mine, because, believe it or not, I had forgotten to give myself one. Actually, that's a lie, I did have one, and it is now in my scrap book of mementos.

Cilla, Bobby and all other guests were by now shown to their seats. The Queen's College quartet was playing while the guests were arriving, and all was ready for the Bride and her grandson to appear. Assembling at the door with the five Bridesmaids in tow, Lilian and grandson followed the Rev. Anthony Grosse up the aisle, who whispered as he neared me 'a piece of cake'. During the service, Susan McCulloch sang her first solo, *One hand, one heart*, accompanied by her personal pianist. The ceremony included the blessing of the rings, and when the service was completed, and we were ready to leave, Susan sang her second solo, *Love changes everything*. We then assembled at the church entrance whilst our photographer, Mike Vaughan took many stills. A photocall for the photographers and television film crews took place  at the same time. Among the photographs taken was what I called a 'confetti throw' picture.

A young boy thrust a small bunch of freshly gathered snowdrops into Lilian's hand. Did he pick them from the churchyard? Upon reaching the open top car, for the benefit of the onlookers and their cameras, Lilian put one foot on the running board and showed off her shapely leg. Pardon, Dear? Oh! I'm sorry, fancy garter.

Now the next venue was one to which I am sure all of the guests were happy to go - the reception at Burnworthy Manor. As becomes the duty of the Bride and Groom, they greeted the guests on arrival. Among those greeted were Cilla and Bobby, who presented us with a lovely wedding present, a silver heart shaped photo frame, engraved with *To Lilian and David with Love from Cilla and Bobby*. A really beautiful gift.

After the meal of excellent food, champagne and wine, Rupert introduced Colin to give the first speech, which was as follows:

'Ladies and Gentlemen, boys and girls, I'd like to start by thanking you all for being here to witness the marriage of Lilian and David. I find myself in the very unusual position of giving away my grandma on a *Blind Date* wedding, it doesn't happen every day, I've been told to look at it as more of gaining a grandad than losing a grandma. As you can probably tell I'm very nervous, which I wasn't until my new grandad told me that fifteen million people will be watching. When my grandma told me that she was going on *Blind Date*, I wasn't at all surprised as she has always wanted to appear on television. When she told me she was marrying I was shocked. But I was also very pleased for her, and having got to know David I know that they will be very happy together. So I'd like to take this opportunity to ask you all to raise your glasses to Lilian and David.'

Cilla was heard to say 'Marvellous'. I am sure that we all thought the same. What a great speech he had made. Lilian was proud too; after all, he is her grandson.

Then it was my turn to make a speech, and it went like this:

'I speak on behalf of my wife Lilian and myself, in welcoming and thanking all our guests here today, and for those who have travelled a long distance from Spain, London, Newcastle and Liverpool, our appreciation for your long journeys. We welcome Lilian's and my relatives, our friends, our celebrities, Cilla and Bobby and members of the *Blind Date* team. Congratulations on the hat, Cilla, blame it on Lilian that you had to have a new one. We are indeed honoured that you have all come here to see Lilian from Newcastle and David from Devon become Mr and Mrs Fensom. We are the proof that two people can, in a very short space of time, become attracted to each other and fall in love. We are indebted to Cilla and her team for bringing us together in happiness, and we are pledged to look after each other in our twilight years. We respect our families and friends, and you will always be welcome. We thank our five lovely bridesmaids, you did a great job, and we hope that we shall be around to be invited to your weddings. Thank you Paul for being my best man, and to Colin for giving away his grandma. For the gifts you have so kindly given us, we thank you sincerely. For the daughters and friends who took so much trouble to arrange for the bridesmaids' dresses, a special thank you. We do appreciate all concerned in making the Blessing in St Mary's church a wonderful occasion, an occasion I am sure will long be remembered in this dear little village of Hemyock. Regretfully, we had to turn down the offer of a pram, had it been a self assembly flat pack we might have made it into two zimmer frames, and the wheels would have come in handy. Please remain seated while Lilian and I drink a toast to you, our dear relatives and friends, and to all those who have contributed so much to make this, our wedding day, such a wonderful occasion. Thank you from the bottom of our hearts. The toast is - Our dear relatives and friends.'

I included in my speech a list of credits to people and organisations who had contributed to the wedding arrangements.

The third and final speech fell to the best man, Paul, a lively and humorous speech which went as follows:

'First of all, a message from Sue and Alex, the first *Blind Date* wedding couple: *Welcome to Britain's most exclusive club, you have just doubled the membership. Seriously, we hope you will have a most fantastic day, we can still remember ours as if it were yesterday. You will have a fabulous time, congratulations to you both and have a wild day.* I don't look upon today as losing a father-in-law but retaining my whisky supply. I think David and I have consumed so much in the past that his marriage has probably saved both our livers. I would like to give Lilian a little bit of advice, don't let David near any home-made elderberry wine, I won't go into details, I daren't, but suffice it to say it took ages to extract him from the brambles in the garden, once we found him! *(Author's note: it was a few years back, it was powerful stuff, this home made wine, but I liked the flavour and had several glasses, followed by a glass of vintage port. The rest I have no knowledge of until I came to, several hours later with an enormous hangover the like of which I would wish never to repeat. Don't worry, Lilian, elderberry wine, especially of the home-made variety, is not on my list of favourite tipples)* I also have to quash one ugly rumour, Lilian and David didn't have to get married.'

Well, the speeches over, the cutting of the cake was filmed. This cake made by Jane Asher was beautiful, as I mentioned previously, and it seemed a shame to cut it, but that is what it was made for.

With most of the formalities over, it was now the turn of a number of guests who had been invited to do so, to meet Cilla in the music room to chat about Lilian and I and our wedding.

The Reverend Tony was the first, and he remarked that he thought he had far more hope for our future than many of the younger couples today.

Georgina and Paul went next. Cilla said that she bought a new 'at because of Georgina, and asked how she persuaded her Dad to go on *Blind Date*. So

Georgina told her the story of how I was driving her mad, doing nothing, so that when she saw the feature in the local paper about the auditions, she told me, and I finally gave in and agreed to go along.

And so it was the turn of Vic and Norman, my fellow competitors, numbers One and Three. When asked, Vic said that he was disappointed that Lilian didn't pick him, but thought that I was the best man for Lilian (Thanks, Vic!). Norman said that he too was disappointed that Lilian didn't pick him, and that if Lilian had picked him, he might well have been in my position today! He then wished us every happiness.

The three youngest bridesmaids, my granddaughters Sophie, Amy and Rebecca all sat together on the sofa, and when asked by Cilla what they would be calling their latest grandma, they all said together, 'Grandma Blind Date.'

Linda, when it was her turn, said that she had not watched the show because she was too embarrassed about her mum, but now that the wedding was over, she would watch it. She said some nice things about me too. Lilian's baby brother, Raymond, sitting beside Linda, when asked by Cilla if he thought I had my hands full with Lilian, said, 'If he doesn't do as he is told he will be in trouble.'

Later it was party time, the disco set up and under way, with many informal photographs taken, plus some nice camcorder shots of Lilian and I with our friends from London Weekend Television. It was then opportune for us to pop into the Manor and change into our *going away* clothes for the filming of the finale.

Robin arrived with his white Rolls, complete with *Just Married* and the inevitable tin cans on the back. Kisses and handshakes and goodbyes all round, we got into the car and drove off with the guests chanting the *Blind Date* theme.

A hundred yards or so down the drive, Robin turned the Rolls and we came back to the party to continue with the festivities and the fun. Our friends were busy packing up their cameras and gear and preparing to leave. It had been a long busy day for them, and I am going to record in this book how much we appreciated them all.

Paul and I had arranged for a bus to collect us from the Manor and to take us to our various destinations, our cars would be collected the following day. It was after midnight when the bus came, and we toured around, ours being the final drop-off.

Now came the opportunity to continue the celebrations until the small hours when we finally gave in.

*What a day this has been,*
*What a great mood we're in,*
*It's lovely just being in love.*
(All lyrics by Lilian)

This book on our wedding and its consequences would not be complete without a feature by Humphrey the house dog, real name Dufosee Galleon of Thorndon, who, after his fifteen years, is now the permanent resident of the basket beside the Aga in the farm kitchen. Poor old fellow, stone deaf, arthritic and with a heart problem, but never a loser. His story, translated by Georgina from Beaglish to English, which I might add was not an easy task, his methods of communication being mainly by the eyes, accompanied by an occasional 'woof' from the throat, and that useful semaphore device cleverly situated at his rear end. His account, if a little selfish, is recorded here: -

**Humphrey the Beagle's eye view of that wedding.**

**January 1993**
Grandpa coming to live in grandpa pad at farmhouse: great news as he really is a soft touch for my head on the lap, appealing look at the table.

**February 1993**
Mum sees advert for *Blind Date* auditions in local paper, and as grandpa is driving her mad, she suggests he try. Grandpa has agreed and has decided a shopping trip to Exeter is needed for something to wear. Oh dear! I think the magic plastic is about to take a bashing.

It did. All togged up ready for the interviews which seems to be successful - phew.

**May 1993**
Second interview - another new outfit . . . again successful.

**August 1993**
Telephone call from *Blind Date*, great excitement, he has been chosen as one of the three men.

**October 1993**
Grandpa off to London for the show. Mum pacing around and hot on every 'phone call - then late evening Grandpa calls to say he's been picked and is off to Jersey for his *date*. Grandpa home now and guess what? He's lovesick, even more of a soft touch.

**November 1993**
Meet Lilian, she is not used to dogs, but likes me - who wouldn't? I ask myself, Beagle of the world, grey, well mannered (sometimes).

**December 1993**
All panic - a wedding! On TV! Girls not wanting to wear bridesmaids' dresses. Dad's going to be best man! Tim refusing point blank to be page boy - Tee Hee! Date fixed for February 5th as Cilla is on holiday in

David (centre) on the set of *Blind Date* with Cilla Black.

Cilla with Lilian on the set of *Blind Date*.

On the settee with Cilla.

The wedding day.

At the reception.

With the Maids of Honour and Miss Jersey
at the Battle of the Flowers, Jersey.

Judging a fashion show.

On board the Canberra.

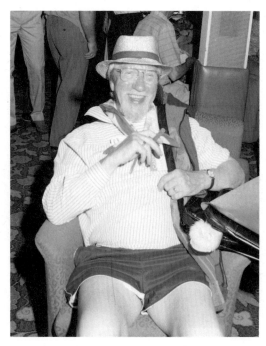

Dressed as 'Abandon Ship' on board the Canberra.

The first Christmas together.

Celebrating the First Wedding Anniversary.

January, and Mum saying it can't possibly clash with Crufts in March.

**January 1994**
Depressed - they don't want a beagle guard of honour at the church. Their loss. Grandpa and Lilian on busy round of TV shows and interviews - the TV and the press have even been coming to the farm - I tried to do my guard beagle bit, but they laughed at me! I'll leave it to the setters in future as that is all they are fit for. *Blind Date* team make huge fuss of us - Dad telephoning regularly from Germany with amendments to his speech.

**February 3rd**
Crew arrive to sort out camera angles in MY kitchen, and, wait for this, Mum, (the turncoat) says that my basket can be moved. Where to? I dread to think!

**February 4th**
*Morning* - Grandpa still very calm. Mum in fit of cleaning and lots of new plants have arrived for the kitchen - shouldn't take her long to kill them off!
*Afternoon* - Lots of friends arriving to stay - when am I going to get my beauty sleep?
*Evening* - All the men (or should I say little boys) dragging grandpa off to the pub, and as soon as the door closes the wine bottles come out and vast quantities are consumed by the women.

*Midnight* - Women go to bed, at last I can have some peace!

*12.30 am* - CRASH! The men return, giggling and shushing, and, goody goody, they are raiding the fridge - time to be on full alert for pickings as they get very sentimental towards me when they have been drinking.

## February 5th

The Saturday of the wedding. 6.30 am - I've only had four hours sleep.

*8.00 am* - John takes children to school, comes home feeling quite unwell - no sympathy!

*8.30 am* - TV crew arrive - I have been warned that if I bark it could be my very last - what do they mean?

All over now, much quicker to clear away, kitchen looks normal, flowers arrive, cars come. Dad and Grandpa go off to Registry Office. Peace. Oh no! Everyone else now getting up, Mum's hair and face all tarted up.

*12.45 pm* - Children arrive home, thrown in bath, fed a snack (I could help). Tim very smart but most uncomfortable, Sophie and Amy have their dresses on and Mum is putting flowers in their hair - I thought they were the things you sidled up to in the garden when nature calls - obviously they are dual purpose.

*1.30 pm* - Everyone leaving for church now, and Tom arrives to house sit. I'm sure he is here just to keep me company and pander to my needs - I think I will show him the fridge first.

*2.00 am* - in the morning - I feel as if I have only just gone to sleep, but oh no! They are all back again, very merry, happy and full - I'm glad someone is because, guess what? They have forgotten to feed me!

Well, what did you think of that, I thought it was great, and I did think of asking Humphrey to sign it, but on second thoughts I remembered that his signature was a one leg up, wee in the shoe job, which he had practised on all four wheels of my car. Once he prepared to sign on the new fridge, but got a smack from his Mistress and thought better of it.

All dogs, as we know, are individual characters, and can be lovable, naughty, selfish, generous, greedy, in fact they can have and be capable of all the same characteristics which we humans are capable of possessing. There are occasions when Humphrey excelled himself, and a couple spring to mind. He was too large to be a lap dog, but that did not stop him from trying, nevertheless, sometimes just curling up on our feet. At the time of my bereavement he was assigned to my bedroom, his bed on the floor alongside mine. He snored terribly through the night, but he was there. I recall one day when his Mistress placed a frozen family sized fresh cream gateau on top of the fridge to thaw whilst we all popped out for a short walk. About half an hour later, when we returned, where was the gateau? Just a smear of chocolate on the fridge door, the box, clean as a whistle, on the floor, not a sign of the cake anywhere. There was Humphrey, curled up in his bed by the Aga, all innocent like, with one eye open, and a stomach like a football. He paid for it though, no dinner for two days, and no tit-bits! The cats loved him, slept in his bed with him, on him and under him, cleaned him as well. What a life of Riley! Sadly, Humphrey will never get to be shown his part in the production of this book. When he could no longer control his rear end, he was relieved of his suffering by a visit from the vet, and now rests in his garden, having left us with fifteen years of his memory.

# Chapter 6

## The Honeymoon

The day following the wedding was spent in preparations for the honeymoon, scheduled to commence on Monday the seventh of February. Jersey Tourist Board, in conjunction with Jersey European Airways and the Hotel L'Horizon had offered us the honeymoon in Jersey, which we had been grateful to accept. What lay in store for us during that honeymoon could not have been foreseen in a lifetime.

Sunday 6th February it poured with rain, similar to the days prior to the wedding day, but we were not concerned - we'd had our day, and the weather could not have been finer for us. We returned to the Manor house to collect our clothes, presents and the remainder of the wedding cake. The rest of the day had been employed in saying goodbye to the departing guests, and packing the cases.

Monday was an early start, catching a taxi to the airport. The formalities concluded, we boarded the plane, to be greeted by the stewardess with a full bottle of champagne, already opened. Although not used to a liquid breakfast, we appreciated the offer. This was luxury indeed, and we shared it with some of our fellow passengers. Lilian had a full glass of the bubbly, and I thought at the time that she might have taken a fancy to it.

It was only a short flight to Jersey, and imagine our surprise when we left the terminal to find our friend with his limousine and his peaked cap. He took us to the hotel.

I had found it very pleasant driving in Jersey with its 40 mph speed limit, and this journey turned out to be no exception. The manager was waiting to greet us for the second time, and we were shown to our accommodation, a beautiful suite of rooms, consisting of a bedroom with television set, canopied bed and en-suite bathroom, a lounge with a three piece suite and television set, plus an adjoining dressing room, which Lilian had collared for herself.

And what had we found on the sideboard? Yes - another bottle of bubbly on ice, plus a huge bouquet of flowers and basket of fruit. The rooms faced the sea, and were equipped with a balcony. Luxury indeed! Am I repeating myself?

A letter awaited us from Emma Pallot, P.R. Executive from Jersey tourism, welcoming us to the island and informing us of the arrangements for our stay.

Europcar offered us a complimentary hire car, a Metro, for our personal use for the week.

Zöe from LWT had telephoned us saying that she would meet us for lunch on the Tuesday, at the Potteries, and that she would be bringing a newspaper reporter who wanted to do a feature on the honeymoon. Then early on the Tuesday morning, a further telephone call came from Zöe saying that she would meet us as arranged, but couldn't stay for lunch as she had to return to the mainland. We were disappointed that the meeting would be short, nevertheless we set off for the potteries as arranged, in the limousine.

Zöe arrived to greet us, then we met Jonathan Jones, who explained about the wedding present they were going to give us. It was a pottery clock, currently in the process of manufacture, and we were required to sign our names on the front before firing. There was a second clock, identical, which we were to sign. This second clock, it turned out, went to a charity, and was the subject of a 'phone-in'. To return to the story, however, as we were signing our names, suddenly the voice of Cilla called out from behind us, 'Lilian and David, surprise! surprise!'

Well, we were completely taken by surprise, there she was, right out of the blue, and then appeared the other members of the *Blind Date* team, the camera and sound men and their equipment.

Cilla went on to say that whilst on the couch after our date, we had mentioned we were considering going on a Mediterranean cruise on the Canberra, but that because we had been busy with our wedding plans, it was a pity that we had missed out, and that she had another blind date for us. The card she gave to Lilian was for a Mediterranean cruise on the Canberra!

We were very emotional at the time, and then Cilla said that we didn't have to come back and tell them all about it, just send a card.

'But we will,' said Lilian.

Cilla then suggested we had a toast, to wish us *bon voyage*. At this point, we asked Cilla if she would like to put her name on the clocks, with ours, which she did.

Sat in the pottery's restaurant, Cilla asked if our feet had touched the ground yet, and Lilian's answer was that we were still on cloud nine.

'What was in your mind when you arrived for the wedding and saw all the crowds lining the streets?' asked Cilla.

'Fantastic,' replied Lilian.

'I thought the road was up,' I said.

'What did you think, David, when you saw Lilian in her wedding dress?' asked Cilla.

'I thought she looked marvellous, and I was so proud,' I answered.

Cilla then said that if that was not enough, she had another little prezzy for us, and that on behalf of the whole *Blind Date* team, they had made a very special wedding album for us. She then gave us this beautiful wedding album, which was full of all the still pictures taken at the wedding and the reception.

'I love surprises, don't you? Go on, give her a kiss, that's enough,' said Cilla.

There followed a filmed scene of Lilian and I walking along the beach, into the distance.

An excellent lunch was waiting for us all back at the hotel, then the time came for them all to leave us on our own.

Words cannot really express our thoughts and feelings about that day, we get very emotional when we re-live those moments. We spent the rest of the day marvelling at our good fortune, and were oblivious to what was happening around us. What had we done to deserve such kindness?

That night we rang our daughters to tell them of our good news, spending about an hour each on the phone. We wanted to spread our excitement into our families, so that they could join with us in marvelling at our good fortune. What we said exactly is impossible to recall, but we knew that they would be sharing our joys, and that they were right behind us in their support. We wanted all the world to know how happy we were. The following day we drove to the local shops for lunch and some shopping.

There being a bus stop outside the hotel, we decided to make use of the local transport to go into town, St.

Helier, and upon entering the bus we were recognised by the driver. Being the only passengers at that time, he very kindly gave us a running commentary on all the places of interest on the journey. It was much more pleasant than driving. He pointed out the position of the Underground German Hospital, and the new leisure centre, as well as other architectural features, the details of which we ask you to excuse us from remembering, considering the whirl of events in which we had become involved. But how kind he was to give us his attention. We have both of us been on conducted tours (not together, I might add) but we were both agreed that this had been one of the best that either of us had experienced, and so unexpected.

Strolling along the streets, looking in the shops, we were stopped by two young ladies who insisted we had a drink with them in the wine bar from whence they had come. They said they were on their lunch break. We must have been in this bar for about three hours, the manager brought out a bottle of champagne, with that and the drinks we bought each other, we must all have been a little merry, in fact we were invited to a children's party, but unfortunately never made it.

Sorry, girls, we were kinda busy, perhaps another time, meanwhile, give our love to the kids, and to yourselves.

We had a telephone call from a lady who introduced herself as Margaret Beadle, who wanted to talk to us about the Jersey *Battle of Flowers*. So we made arrangements to meet her. A message was left at reception for us to return a call to a Senator, Terry Le Mann. We returned the call, and he invited us to a luncheon. It so happened that this clashed with our meeting with Margaret, but Terry said not to worry, she would be there too. Friends of theirs picked us up in their car, and we arrived at this hotel to find that it was a luncheon for the 'Over Forties Club', and that eighty guests were there. We had an excellent lunch; Terry made a speech welcoming us. He presented us with a gift of pottery, an exquisite piece, a little child bending over looking into a doll's house. It was then that Margaret asked us if we were willing to come to Jersey again, in August, to judge at the *Battle of Flowers*. The prospect of that was exciting, and we readily agreed - it would fit in nicely with our programme for the coming summer months, the cruise in July, and Jersey in August. Margaret then took us to meet a friend of hers, Teddy Knowles.

A drive into St Aubin, we parked and walked along the sea front. As we were passing a beauty salon, a man who introduced himself as Adrian called after us to 'come in and have a spray'. Well, we did so, and Lilian came out of the shop with a bag full of perfume samples. Next we paid a visit to a gift shop along the road, to purchase gifts to take home for our grandchildren, and he gave us a generous discount.

What kind people we had met in Jersey. St Aubin is one of the places which we would be visiting again, and would become one of our favourites. One lady shot across the road in her car, almost on to the pavement to call out and wish us luck. It was amazing, we had become famous!

The day before we left for home, we had a horse and carriage ride laid on for us by Jersey tourism. Emma explained that they had wanted to do this for us when we were over on the *Date* in October, but due to weather conditions it was not possible. We thoroughly enjoyed the two hour trip in an elegant carriage with two great horses. It was very cold, but we snuggled up with blankets to combat the keen wind.

We were due to arrive early, in order for the programme to link up with GMTV. It was a special put on for Valentine's day, and the studio was opened up early in order to get the programme across on time. This meant that the crew had to arrive before their normal work hours. However, it did not take long for them to get themselves organised, and us briefed as to what was required from us. This consisted of a general discussion about the wedding, how we had enjoyed the honeymoon, stuff like that. A very enjoyable interview, everybody being so kind.

A short visit to the television studio early in the morning was set up, in order for us to do an interview.

Sadly, it was time for us to return to the mainland, and our friend with his limousine was there to take us. Whilst waiting in the terminal, a gentleman came over to us, introduced himself as a Director of the Airport, and said that he had been speaking with a Director from the BBC, and that he was a worried man, because we had sixteen million viewers. Phew!

Margaret came to the terminal to see us off and to give us a parting gift, a beautiful pottery figure. It was now goodbye for the present. Arriving at Exeter we were met by four newspaper reporters anxious for a story, and it was there that a public relations lady from Jersey European Airways also met us and gave Lilian a huge bouquet of fresh flowers. A taxi laid on by Chris took us home.

We now had time to reflect and consider all that had taken place on our honeymoon. How fortunate we had been. So many nice things, and so much to look forward to. What we had thought would have been a quiet week together had turned out to be so fantastic, beyond our most imaginative dreams. All our relatives and friends were anxious to know all about our honeymoon, and to peruse the magnificent album full of wedding photographs, given to us by Cilla. Even at this stage in our relationship we could not envisage that we would be caught up in a whirlwind of engagements and publicity that would be with us for an indefinite period. So be it! We were not complaining, just feeling thankful for the kindness we were experiencing from so many quarters.

# Chapter 7

## The Fishing Weekend at Eggesford

Gordon Cleaver, the Economic Development Officer of Mid Devon District Council, who negotiated the arrangements for the *Glorious Getaways* holiday break, with David Ingyon, the owner of the Fox and Hounds Hotel, did offer to assist with our travel arrangements, but we thought that we should make the effort and arrive under our own steam. This turned out to be a rather unwise decision on our part, beautiful though that region of the country is. Lilian called it an horrendous journey, particularly as she had forgotten to take her knitting, and travelwise she is not particularly good on twisting and turning country roads. I wouldn't put it so strongly as that, but then I am not particularly good at direction finding. We had covered quite a few miles before I came to the conclusion that we were going in the opposite direction. I didn't admit to it however, but explained that it was the scenic route. That excuse did not go down very well, but then, after all, what did it matter? We didn't have a train or a flight to catch, and were expected when we arrived. Which we did of course, otherwise I wouldn't be writing about it, would I?

It was early afternoon when we arrived, to be greeted by our hosts Sheila and David. After congratulations and drinks, we were shown to our room, resplendent with a huge lace adorned four poster bed. We could definitely see that this was the honeymooners' room, particularly as in one corner there was what Lilian called the *huffy* bed, where no doubt the husband would be despatched should he commit some small misdemeanour or temporarily fall out of favour. We had no use for this contraption, it so happened. After a change of clothing a walk in the country lanes before the evening meal to work up an appetite was decided upon. It was to be a fishing weekend, but at present the conditions were not right, there having been so much rain. The river was chocolate coloured and fast running, not ideal for fishing for the salmon and trout which I was told were in abundance. Indeed, there was a salmon proudly on display in the hotel that another fisherman had recently caught, which I believe was in the region of ten pounds in weight. Nevertheless we thoroughly enjoyed the evening meal and the excellent wine. After retiring into this huge four poster, contrary to common belief, the top did not come down and smother us and tip us into some secret panel, that we might finish up as fish bait! Instead we had a jolly good night's rest, so there.

The next day, Sunday, the weather had not improved, so a drive out led us to a quiet little restaurant for lunch, followed by a trip around a garden centre which we had discovered, resulting in the purchase of gifts and plants etc. Wonderfully exciting stuff of course, but what about all this fishing we were supposed to be doing? Lilian was very pleased with the day, and we both enjoyed another good meal before once again sampling *the* bed. I had forgotten to weigh myself before coming away, just as well perhaps.

Came Monday morning, Gordon and a photographer had been expected, and when they arrived it was decided that I should be introduced to the art of fly fishing right away. I was decked out in a pair of wellies, wearing David's best fishing jacket, which had lots of little flaps with hooks and flies of varied hues and sizes. And of course David's hat, also adorned with flies, feathers, hooks, you name it, it was on there. Lilian couldn't stop laughing when she saw me. How cruel! This was dead serious stuff this.

It put me in mind of the first (and the last) time that I had fished. I was ten years of age at the time, had all the right gear, not the safety pin and string variety, and Dad and I set off for the day complete with bread paste for the bait, to a disused quarry where we had been assured fish were in abundance. Perhaps I should have tried again, but I didn't. I was, you might say, a little disenchanted with the result of my whole day's effort, so ended my hobby. But wait - here I was, sixty one years later, about to re-kindle the enthusiasm. In other words, I was about to have another bash. Lilian excused herself from taking part in the actual business, but instead preferred to be the spectator, as she put it. She was not suitably equipped for 'messing about on the river': a trifle unkind don't you think, to describe such an art in this fashion?

Julian, David's fisheries manager then accompanied me to the edge of the river Taw, and instructed me in the casting of the line, then pulling of the line to keep the fly moving. It was really exciting and I enjoyed it immensely, though it was a shame that I didn't catch anything. I expect the fish must have realised that I was inexperienced, and ignored my fly. Lilian, standing watching with Gordon, alongside the jeep, was quite happy as a spectator. She couldn't stop laughing at my hat, but she was willing for us to have our photographs taken together, including the hat. Later, Gordon did send us copies of those photographs, and Lilian said that those taken of me and the hat were good, but I preferred those which included Lilian.

The time came to bid goodbye to our hosts and Gordon, and to thank them all for the great time. But it wasn't quite over. On the way home we stopped at a supermarket and purchased the biggest whole salmon in the store. Before putting it in the freezer, Lilian took a couple of pictures of me holding this salmon, one with it still in its wrapper, and one with it *in the flesh*. After all, I wouldn't want to create a wrong impression. We did have a smashing weekend.

It has not been possible to write very much about a two day holiday, had I caught a fish, no doubt you may have been bored by the account I would have possibly written. Yes, I was disappointed that I had not, but it was not surprising really, my past experience in these matters being somewhat limited. Perhaps if I had read up the subject of fly fishing beforehand (Isn't there a book on the subject much advertised on the TV?), maybe even if I had gone on a trial or a practice course, assuming that I had had the time, I might have had more success. I would say this much, however, if the opportunity occurred again to participate in some fly fishing, I would jump at the chance. Also, I feel sure that in the short time I learned enough to stand me in good stead. I may even decide to get myself a rod and a hat.

# Chapter 8

## Mediterranean Cruise on the Canberra.

*Anchors aweigh, my lads,*
*Anchors aweigh,*
*It's Lilian and David's happy holiday.*
(Lyrics again by Lilian)

Have you, the reader, ever been on a cruise? If you have, you will know what I am writing about, and you will probably agree with my feelings about the subject. If you have not had that experience, then what I am about to describe could make you feel envious, or could prompt you to dash out and secure your passage on one of the many cruises which are on offer to the public. I know that our particular cruise, which Cilla Black so kindly gave to us on our Jersey honeymoon, was a wedding gift from London Weekend Television and P. & O. Cruises, so that my expenditure was minimal in comparison with the normal outlay required when going on a luxury sea voyage, but I can assure you that our happy introduction to this type of holiday was so good that it would not be a *one off*, as you will discover when you reach the end of this chapter.

Due to the particular circumstances of this holiday, some special provision had been made prior to our embarkation. We were requested to be at the Southampton terminal some two hours before the usual time that passengers were due to arrive. Nina Donaldson, assistant producer for LWT's *Blind Date* had arranged to meet us, together with Mike Vaughan, photographer, and two of P. & O.'s Public Relations lady representatives, for a photo-call.

Having left our car, as arranged, with Andrews Shipside Services, who stored it during the voyage, our luggage was taken by porters to our cabin. Being a little earlier that the pre-arranged time, we chatted to a couple who introduced themselves as Mike's Mum and Dad. So when Nina arrived with Mike, and the two P. R. ladies as well, Mike took pictures of us all together. Nina gave Lilian a huge bunch of flowers, which was from Cilla and the *Blind Date* team. Those flowers graced the table in our cabin for the whole voyage, and were regularly watered by our kind cabin steward.

There followed many photographs of us together in various situations around the ship, and in particular we were invited to join Captain Ian Gibb on the bridge, where there were some really memorable shots taken, some with a glass of champagne in our hands. The time arrived for Nina and Mike's departure, so with streamers from us to the shore, the last pictures were taken by Mike, and they left us, two happy people on the eve of a wonderful experience. We couldn't really believe what had happened. Were we dreaming? Was it just our imagination running wild?

Lots of fellow passengers had by this time arrived, and we had a whale of a time with them, their cameras and camcorders, so many wanting to take home memories of our meeting with them.

Our cabin number determined that we would be allocated to the Pacific restaurant, and we chose the early sitting for the meals. As we had made the choice, the invitation we had from the Captain to be on the Bridge when the Canberra left Southampton had to be regretfully declined as it coincided with the evening meal. However Captain Gibb told us that he would make it up to us when we reached Gibraltar.

This first meal, of seven courses, accompanied by a good bottle of wine (we weren't driving home) was great, and a taste of what we had to come. We had been allocated a table for two in a corner, alongside a table for four, our fellow guests, with whom we spent many happy hours together during our voyage. They were Derek and Ann, Len and Ivy, from Rochdale. What a small world it is - when discussing the *Blind Date* show with them, they mentioned they had a friend, Donna, also from Rochdale, who had been on one of the shows. She had in fact been on at the same time as us, and had a great time with her date, Eddy from Ilford.

Our waiter, Andrew, looked after our table for the whole of the cruise, and helped to make it so perfect.

We had made many friends on the voyage, including Dawn and Mark from Kent, with whom we still correspond.

A ship's newspaper appeared in our cabin every evening, informing us of progress, destination arrival times and what's on, plus the suggested dress of the day, be it informal, casual or formal, a very useful guide for men and women. We had been advised of the 'Black and White' night, fancy dress night, etc.

For the fancy dress night, Lilian presented herself as 'Turkish Delight', complete in costume, yashmak and a *Turkish Delight* chocolate on a velvet cushion. Can you imagine the fun she had making those curled over slippers? I had not intended to take part, to the chagrin of Lilian and friends, so, in the spirit of the thing, I disappeared to the cabin, and returned as 'abandon ship', with shirt and shorts on back to front, odd socks, odd shoes, ladies' scarf with tucked in toothbrush, cigar, Panama hat and a P. & O. travel bag with one of Lilian's pink fluffy slippers hanging out.

The idea had come to me when, at the Captain's newcomer meeting, he had discussed a certain signal on the ship's siren, which was to summon everybody to assemble at given points throughout the ship, and was not a signal to abandon ship. The judges must have felt sorry for me, because I won a bottle of bubbly. But I still think Lilian would have deserved it more than I did (I'm a crawler).

It did not take us long to get used to the superb food (blow the diet). We had decided to enjoy it, even if it meant that we need not eat for a month when we got back home!

For the 'Black and White' night, Lilian chatted up Andrew for some paper doilies and a paper plate, made a hat with the plate, cut up the doilies and sewed them all round the hem of her black dress. It looked great, and in the photograph we had taken together after, it looked really professional. I had no problems with mine, black trousers with white tuxedo, white shirt and black tie, but there again Lilian took a hand and fashioned for me a black rose buttonhole, made from a silk handkerchief. There's no end to her talents (do you want your trousers shortened or a new zip?) I could go on, but her modesty forbids me.

Along with the other newcomers, we were invited to a welcoming cocktail party attended by the Captain and his other officers.

Gibraltar was our first port of call, and we had booked a tour which took us up into the rocky caves, and met the apes, cheeky animals, who, we were told, were very partial to handbags and cameras. The tour terminated in the town, and Lilian, straight out of the coach, was across the road in a flash, into the first shop she saw for gifts to take home. We repeated this procedure on a number of occasions, being interrupted frequently by other holidaymakers who expressed their desire to congratulate us on our marriage. Now wasn't that nice of them? And it did cut down a bit on Lilian's trolley dash, ho-ho!

Upon returning to the ship, waiting in our cabin was the Captain's invitation to the Bridge. True to his word, we witnessed the Ship's departure from this excellent vantage point, we just had to keep out of the Pilot's and Navigating Officers' way. There was very limited space for the turn around, assisted by two tugs, one at the bow and the other at the stern, push pull. That manoeuvre completed, we headed out to sea, accompanied by the music from the Band of The Royal Corps of Signals. We had taken the opportunity to write numerous postcards, an occurrence which repeated itself all the way on the voyage. Lilian, bless her, had an appetite for writing postcards and letters which had no bounds, I can tell you without fear of contradiction that in our short married life together, postage stamps have cost us many pounds. One of her little manias is thank you cards, she even sends them to me, if I've done something very nice, although I must say she doesn't post them, just leaves them around for me to find. Ah! that's love, that is.

Now where was I? Before I proceed too far with this account of our cruise, I must stress that this story is about the highlights of our memories, not a blow-by-blow account of the whole twelve days, I wouldn't want to bore the pants off you. There were many activities on board, most of which we did not participate in, but no way is this a criticism, as the company stated in its brochure, you could do as much or as little as you liked. It was this complete freedom of choice which helped to make this cruise such a relaxing and enjoyable one. Again, we wanted to pass on to you these highlights that you may enjoy reading them, and they are not in strict chronological order.

Here's an interesting story about our tour in Italy, to the medieval hill town of Monte Carlo in the Tuscan countryside, well known for its vineyards and fine wines. Not to be confused with the other famous Monte Carlo. After a visit to this small sleepy town, I say sleepy because I can only remember seeing two people, the coach took us on to a vineyard in Lucca, a vineyard wrapped in beauty, its magnificent gardens, and its cool cellars wherein were the large wine vats. We were asked not to make any loud noise, which might be detrimental to the wine making process. We were not told what in fact it would do to the wine if one coughed or sneezed, but assumed they knew what they were talking about.

Fourteen of us were ushered into this room to take part in the wine tasting. I know there were fourteen because I had counted them before the procedure commenced. Now, I had been to wine tasting before, in Italy and other countries. It normally consisted of half a glass of the red and the same with the white variety before being shown into the shop department. But this was something else, it was the best wine tasting that I had ever attended. The table was set with plates and glasses, and six opened bottles on the table. It seemed that we were expected to drink it all, which we did, accompanied by tit-bits and delicacies which they served to us whilst we sampled their excellent wines (I particularly liked the red, I'm very partial to a good full-bodied red wine, I might add) and when we had disposed of those on the table, we were asked to try a clear sweet liquid, which I could honestly say that I don't remember if it were a wine, a spirit or a liqueur.

I cannot speak for the others of course, but I left that table in a very happy frame of mind, having consumed my full share of the red wine, the white wine, the water and that other nice liquid, and after entering the sales department, purchased wine and a bottle of their extra virgin olive oil, this olive oil proved to be an asset in the kitchen.

Now Lilian's capacity and taste for wine is strictly limited to one or even half a glass at one sitting. I cannot condemn her for that, and I am sure there are many people who would praise and even envy her in this. She knows her own limitations, and in no way did I, or would I, make any attempt to change her, not that it would be possible, anyway. She has a remarkable capacity for other things in life, particularly in the field of writing personal letters. Why therefore should I try to influence her? In fact I am grateful that she has firm ideas regarding her intake of any form of alcohol. She doesn't smoke, either, passive smoking makes her cough, so I always try to ensure that we dine in a non-smoking area in a restaurant. I myself admit to enjoying an occasional cigar, but can go for weeks without even thinking about a smoke, then suddenly I get the urge and buy a packet. I try, however, in one of my infrequent cigar smoking sessions, to ensure that it does not inconvenience my dear Lilian. And as for smoking in my car, that is definitely taboo.

It was time to return to the coach to continue our return journey back to the ship. I did notice that as we had passed the leaning tower of Pisa in the distance, it appeared to be leaning over a little further. Now on board the coach there was a female courier, whose task was to give a running commentary on the particular aspects of the countryside through which we passed. I had fallen asleep, and at one stage I had opened my eyes, there was the courier chattering away, and the only people I could see were awake were herself and the driver. Poor kid! I felt sorry for her, this was probably a regular occurrence with this particular journey. But my sorrow was short lived, I fell asleep again.

Much of our time on board was spent in the reclining chairs by the pools. Lilian, being a sun-lover, my job was to slosh on the barrier cream, and as she wasn't wearing very much, I took care to ensure that all exposed parts were properly protected. I myself preferred to keep in the shade or keep exposed parts loosely covered, having had prickly heat on some other occasion, and not wishing to endure the discomfort again. But the weather was so good, one had to take advantage, and we did. I was quite happy with a cool drink, or an ice cream, which was served daily by the pools.

We had met the Captain on a number of occasions, and he always found time to speak, or at the least to give us a smile as he passed, and on one occasion he had said to me, 'When you are fed up with Lilian, David, I'll have her!'

Sorry, Ian, but she still holds that place in my heart. But we both appreciated the thought, I am sure that Lilian did, anyway.

I vividly remember the Hawaiian night, most wearing floral shirts and blouses, we were all decked out with garlands round our necks, just like the players in *South Pacific*. And then there was the carnival night, what a hoot! Cables had been stretched across the pool, part of the pool was boarded over to allow room for the cabaret acts to perform. It was late, the night was dark, the scene being illuminated by the coloured lights around the pool. The deck was crowded, we had all been given packets of streamers, and at a given sign we threw them, aiming to get them over the stretched wires. It was an amazing sight, all these streamers cascading down in a maze of colour.

At most ports of call, when it was not possible to berth the ship, the ship's own launches ferried the passengers to and from the quayside, operating all the time passengers were ashore.

Monte Carlo, the playground for the rich, beautiful weather, beautiful yachts in the bay. Sigh! Beautiful scenery, in my case I was appreciative of the female variety, and which brought to mind Lilian's first question on the *Blind Date* programme, about her dressing up, and what outfit should she wear to turn us on. My answer was 'three first class postage stamps, strategically placed, which would give me a mail advantage'. Well I never thought at that time that I would one day see an outfit as near to that description as was possible. Ee by gum!

Our intention when we arrived at Monte Carlo was to spend a few bob at the casino, but we were in no hurry, just enjoying each other's company whilst walking in the direction which we had been told led towards the cash throw-away facility that we had in mind.

'My mother would like to meet you,' said this lady to us as we passed a roadside restaurant, so we stopped and went to meet her mum, and a number of her relatives who were there. We spent a good couple of hours chatting away like long-lost friends. It was lovely there, sipping coffee, completely relaxed. I did ask if they were from the Canberra, to be told, 'Canberra? No, we have just flown here to Monte Carlo for the weekend.'

Well, we never did get to that casino, but who cares, good conversation is much better than lining some millionaire's pocket.

I must admit to a stroke of luck at the roulette wheel on the Canberra. When my colleague from Rochdale put some money in my hand and said, 'Put a bit on with that,' well I did just that: it won and I gave him the seven quid. Not bad, eh?

It happened that my birthday fell at the latter end of the cruise. Lilian had ordered a cake from the Purser's office, Andrew brought it in, with its one candle alight, and *Happy Birthday* was sung by those in our proximity. Cards came from our friends, one from the Captain, and a signed menu card from Andrew, and of course a kiss and a card from my dear Lilian.

Time passed quickly, and we were on our way back to Southampton. Every evening we had tried to ensure that we did one or two circuits around the deck, twice if we felt energetic enough to make it, before turning in. We both found it to be very relaxing, also, in the evening, to stand leaning on the handrail, listening to the soft throb of the engines below, and watching the bow wave disappearing into the night. Cor!

When we awoke on the morning of arrival, we were already at berth, and our cases had to be outside the cabin door for off-loading. After breakfast, and departure formalities completed, it was goodbye to our fellow passengers, and on to the quayside, Lilian carrying her white Canberra teddy. We collected our baggage and our car, and then back to Devon and home.

> *A life on the ocean wave,*
> *It's lovely to be at sea,*
> *A life on the ocean way,*
> *It is for David and me.*
> (lyrics by guess who! )

We arrived home, sun burned and happy, and I'll tell you of our priority: a telephone call to a travel agent to book a cruise on the, wait for it, yes - the Canberra. When? Christmas and New Year 1995-1996. That is something we have to look forward to.

We had been home for a few days, when we received a large package, a photograph album sent to us by Nina from LWT, full of the pictures taken by Mike prior to our sailing, a great album, and inscribed in gold lettering on the cover *David & Lilian, Canberra 1994, Blind Date*

Thank you, Cilla and your team.

# Chapter 9

## Battle of Flowers

This visit to Jersey was the third in our short life together, first the date, then the honeymoon, and now the Battle.

We had been invited by Margaret Beadle, Vice President of the Battle of Flowers Association, to act as judges in this annual festival, and which we had been very proud to accept.

Friday 5th of August we travelled by air from Exeter Airport, to be met by Margaret and taken to the La Haule Manor Hotel in St Aubin's bay, where we stayed during our visit to the Island. Fellow judges were Buster Merryfield, Uncle Albert from *Only Fools and Horses*, and his wife Iris, also staying in the same hotel. We had great times and laughs with them and thoroughly enjoyed their company. Tony Hardman, P. R. Officer for Bournemouth Coucil's Entertainment Department, was also staying in the hotel, and many of the events were shared with him. Buster and I discovered that during our earlier working days, both in the City of London, we visited the same swimming baths during our lunch break, Goulston Street baths, Aldgate, which is no longer there.

Before our evening meal with Margaret and friends, Lilian and I took a walk along the beach opposite the hotel, and we passed Colette's Cabin, which is actually on the beach, and where she dispenses tea, coffee, ice cream and light meals. We often called in for a coffee and a chat whilst in Jersey. It was here that Colette first spoke to us, and asked if we would be willing to judge children's sand castles on the beach the coming Sunday. *The Daily Mirror* was sponsoring the children's entertainment, and we were all for it. We did say, however, that being in Jersey for a specific function, we would seek Margaret's confirmation that it would not interfere with our programme. When we had the all-clear from Margaret, we accepted Colette's request.

That evening Margaret took us to dinner, where we met her relatives, Bill and Chris, and Amy from the United States. We also met and were introduced to Tony Perkins, Vice President of the Battle Association, and Olaf, producer of the Battle video. It was a most enjoyable evening and a get-to-know-each-other event. On the Saturday morning we had an engagement with the Battle of Flowers Association fête, a grand affair with bands, sideshows and the like. A number of celebrities were there when we arrived, and together with Lionel Blair, Su Pollard and Vicki Michelle, we were introduced over the loud speaker system. There followed an autographing session in aid of charity. Su embraced Lilian and said to her, 'My Mum loves you.'

I told Lionel that one of Lilian's ambitions had been to dance with him, whereupon he took Lilian in a dancing pose, and I was able to take a great photograph of them together. As it was still quite early in Lilian's and my relationship together, I was not aware of all her ambitions, or how many she had realised, but no doubt I would be finding out in due course. I would mention that later, we did send Su a photograph of our wedding for her to give to her Mum, with our love.

It was a most enjoyable day, the weather was fine, and we had fun signing programmes for many happy people. It was followed by another great evening meal with Margaret and friends.

Now it was Sunday, the day of the sand castles on the beach, and to all those children who participated, and I expect their Mums and Dads, it was a very serious matter. After all, how many of us as kids have had the opportunity to show off our prowess as a budding architect, and be rewarded with goodies for our efforts? The prizes were not as grand as a trip for two to Spain, or even a cruise on the Canberra, but who can measure the pleasure of a child who can boast with pride that 'I won a prize for my sandcastle'?

One of the biggest efforts had to be disqualified, as the creators of this enormous heap of castellated sand were in the older child bracket, eighteen to twenty, which in our estimation gave them an unfair advantage over their fellow competitors. But if you meet us again, we'll treat you to your bag of sweeties. Now we can't be fairer than that, can we?

All of the kids made a jolly good effort, and we had to be careful where we put our feet. One of the exhibits proudly presented by one small chap, which consisted of one upturned bucketful of sand with a lollipop stick in the top, had been erected dangerously near to my foot. Top marks for effort, I took a picture of that one with some of the others. After our deliberations, the top three winners were nominated, and they duly got their bag of goodies. All the children got prizes anyway, loads of tee shirts of all sizes were distributed, even I got one. In fact I was given more than one, and Lilian was given enough for all of the grandchildren. Our new friend from *The Daily Mirror* treated us to a great lunch at La Haule Manor, and with a few glasses of wine to celebrate we all agreed it was a great day. Somehow I had acquired what I can best describe as a brilliant red warehouse coat, with *The Daily Mirror* printed right across the back. I wear it when washing the car now - where's my fee for the advertising?

That evening we were invited to the Yacht club for dinner. We believed that an organised trip had been arranged for us, a boat trip, and myself, being an ex Mateolot, this had an appeal that was not to be taken lightly. However, due to circumstances of which we were unaware, this trip had been cancelled, and instead we spent a while in the yacht club bar, indulging in pleasantries with our hosts and fellow guests, before sitting down to an excellent meal. The restaurant was situated in a beautiful position at the water's edge, with a panoramic view across the bay. Way up on the hill opposite there was a lone cottager where, we were told, lived an elderly lady all on her own. We were also told that a gentleman visited her during the winter to take her bread and milk.

Monday morning gave us free time to wander off to the shops along the sea front, and to call in to Adrian's salon for a chat and to show him our photographs of the wedding. He was delighted to see us again, even though we seemed to have halted all his activities with his customers. They didn't seem to mind, though, and just joined in the conversation.

Upon reflection, there are many things we like about Jersey, but most of all it is the people, their friendliness, their kindness, and the happiness which seems to pervade throughout the island. It's no wonder that we seem to be ever going back there. It's not that we find difference on the mainland, we can only speak as we find, and we have met so much kindness, and yes, love as well, from the many folk whom we meet as well as those who write to us. I know that I have mentioned this before, and I will most probably mention it again, but I am determined to get my message across. There are so many millions of nice people out there, and we only tend sometimes to learn about the dodgy ones.

Now where was I? Oh yes, I was walking with my Lilian, when we came to the gift shop owned by Mr and Mrs Fleuret, and popped in to say hello again.

During the afternoon, the judging started in earnest, in this case for the best decorated shop window. We had each been given a list of the entries submitted, and with our judge's badges hung around our necks, made the rounds, making our observations as we moved from one to the other. One particular entry we both remember very well, was the window of the Jersey Cancer Relief charity shop, the staff of which had gone to a lot of trouble in producing a display depicting Mr and Miss Battle together with attendants, models in cream coloured costumes, and with an abundance of flowers. I can say that their efforts were rewarded when it came to the judging, and I saw later a notice in their window informing the public of the result of their achievement. Congratulations from Lilian and myself!

I want also to say that although I have mentioned only one entry, the standard of all the entries was high in my opinion, and it would not be fair of me if I did not include them in my congratulations, so well done, it was a joy to see them.

The following day, Tuesday, we had to visit the hotels and guest houses to view their class of entries in a floral competition. There were a number of these, and it took a while for us to visit them all. I ought to mention that we were not the only judges on any of these occasions: the shops, the hotels and the guest houses, but were members of a party who were all assigned to these tasks. Again Lilian and I were appreciative of the standard of the entries, and there was enthusiasm from all when we arrived to view their efforts. There was one exception however, when we arrived we were met with a blank look, we weren't expected! Not to worry, there were plenty of entries for us all to consider when it came to the crunch, and we put our heads together to decide the eventual order of merit. Whilst having a break, it began to rain. Margaret disappeared for some minutes and returned with a pink sweatshirt for Lilian, with the Jersey logo on it, to protect Lilian's bare shoulders from the weather. Now that's what I recognise as kindness, and that's Margaret.

Wednesday was another free day until the evening, when we attended the Town Hall, for the *Vin d'Honneur* with Margaret, Buster and Iris. It was here that we met and were introduced to Ian Botham with his wife and family. Also, Tony Hardman introduced us to the Lieutenant Governor, Air Chief Marshal Sir John Sutton, and his wife.

Imagine Lilian's and my surprise when we were called forward to receive a commemoration for our part in the judging, a cut glass vase inscribed *Jersey Battle of Flowers Association Mr and Mrs D Fensom Judges*

*1994*. Buster and Iris had one too. Ours has its place in our showcase, alongside our wedding presents. We were very thankful for this, just to be there would have been sufficient reward.

A visit to some of the float exhibitors' workshops was the next stage, where the finishing touches were being put to their entries. What enthusiasm, what a lot of sheer hard work was being put into their projects. Dozens of people were in each shed, each with an allotted task, many trimming the flowers, of which there were bunches and bunches in vases, each head being individually examined and trimmed, before being glued or fixed to the subject. The sheer size and complexity of the undertaking deserved admiration, as well as the volunteers dutifully and cheerfully carrying out their part of the operation. It was lovely to talk to them, most of whom knew who we were, so we had no problems introducing ourselves. We understood that some of the drivers of the floats would be hidden from view, and that control of the steering and speed would be by walkie-talkie from somebody walking in front of the float. These large floats were not mounted on the backs of lorries, but had their own chassis, with the engine somewhere below, out of sight. No small undertakings these, but splendid examples of sheer determination.

Lilian and I will always remember how privileged we were to see so much and to feel so involved in it all. I myself could have stayed for hours watching all this feverish activity, but we were on our way again, this time to the Pomme d'Or Hotel for a reception.

Thursday, the day of the Battle had arrived. Margaret collected us all in her car, and took us to the *La Belle Fleur* enclosure, the V.I.P. stand on the Battle route, where we had been allocated seats in the front row. Before the parade commenced, however, we attended a lunch in the hospitality marquee behind the stand. All seats were reserved, and our fellow diners at our table were Max and Blossom Bygraves, Mr and Mrs Ray, Margaret and Tony, and Buster and Iris. An excellent lunch was served, and we had the pleasure of meeting Jimmy White, Su Pollard, Vicki Michelle and Les Dennis and his fiancée, Amanda, now his wife. After lunch, we took our seats in preparation for the Battle parade.

We had all been given large bags of confetti to chuck about, which we proceeded to do forthwith. More bags were forthcoming, and when I tell you that at the end of the day the floor was more than one inch deep in the stuff, I am not exaggerating.

We had a wonderful view from where we sat, in the front row of the V.I.P. stand, it was all going on right out there in front of us. It has to be seen to be believed, the pageantry, the music, the colours. Mere words cannot convey the splendour of it all.

Buster rode in one of the cars, but Iris remained with us. When the float, an open topped bus, of the Good

Companions Club came alongside, one of the ladies, Marion, alighted, rushed up the stairs and embraced Lilian and I, to the cheers of her friends on the float. Great stuff again, this! Whilst sitting there we were both interviewed by Channel TV.

As the last of the procession disappeared along the route, we descended once more into the marquee, covered in confetti, for tea and cakes. Then it was back to the hotel, shedding confetti like serious dandruff, to prepare for the evening meal.

Perhaps it was my imagination, or did we have more evening dinners than there were days? Fortunately I had a good appetite, still have, I am pleased to say, but you, the reader, do not wish to know that, I am sure.

The venue was the Lobster Pot, a well known restaurant, good food and wine again. Lilian danced with Tony (he's a better dancer than I am) and I believe we had a bit of a sing song as well, but you will know of my efforts at a sing song if you saw Lilian and I on our *Blind Date* show, so I won't say any more about that.

Friday was a free day until the evening, when we returned once more to the V.I.P. stand, this time to witness the Moonlight Parade. This spectacular event was the Battle all over again, but this time with a difference: all the floats were illuminated with thousands of coloured lights, and that coupled with the mechanical movements, some with imitation smoke coming from them, was not to be missed. As it was now dark, the show had a new enchantment.

A fireworks display laid on completed the evening's entertainment. But not for us, off we went to an evening meal at the Cristina Hotel.

We had heard that this Hotel commanded the best view of the Island of Jersey, over St Aubin's Bay. The food and the wine were superb, and the service impeccable. It was overall a very exciting and enchanting experience. Both Lilian and I were enthralled, and, together with our Host, Margaret, thoroughly enjoyed the evening.

The following day, Saturday, all the exhibits were on view to the public, before being taken away for dismantling, and the redesigning of the exhibits for the following year. That says much for the dedication of all those involved in this great venture, the planning for the next year has already commenced. A sixteen page print out entitled 'The Battle of Flowers '94 Year of the Dragon' which was published, gave a full account of the show, and the comments from a number of personalities interviewed. They published our picture and our comments as follows: 'TV's Blind Date Couple Lilian and David Fensom, returning to their honeymoon Island, 'It's beyond belief. It's more than we expected. It's only when you see them on the parade you realise all the hard work that has gone into making the floats.'

We visited the Jersey Hospital fête, which Buster, Lilian and I formally opened. We all said a few words each, Buster with his humour, kicked off, so to speak, I added a few words and Lilian said, 'Have a nice day'. We had a great time meeting people, especially the nurses, and who did we bump into? It was Terry Le Main, Senator, whom we had met whilst on our honeymoon.

However the visit was drawing to a close. There was one more function to attend, which was the Exhibitors' Presentation night at the Skyline, Hotel de France. Another memorable occasion when the winners received their prizes.

Sunday, back to the airport, time for a coffee in the restaurant before leaving. Then it was goodbyes and into the departure lounge. It was while we were sitting there waiting to board that a stewardess approached Lilian and said to her,

'Who's a naughty girl then?'

She explained that Lilian had left her handbag on the back of a chair in the restaurant. Oh dear! Fortunately, a waitress had noticed, and knew that Lilian had been sitting on that chair. For security reasons the bag had to be retained until we had boarded the plane. It wasn't until we were seated awaiting take-off that the bag was delivered by special van, and brought to Lilian by a stewardess while she was sitting in her seat. I had imagined that if the said bag had not been identified as belonging to Lilian, security would spring into action. I had visions of the bag being placed in a bucket in the middle of a field by one of those robot machines, and detonated. It would have played havoc with her pension book and her lipstick, not to mention the bag itself, which was a present to Lilian from me.

It put me in mind of when we were on a train from London, after one of our visits, when a message came over the intercom requesting that the owner of a cardboard box left on the counter of the restaurant car, come forward to claim it. After another couple of repeat requests, the train stopped at Reading station and all passengers in the vicinity, about two carriages either side of the restaurant car, were asked to leave the train, leaving our baggage behind. What happened after that I cannot be sure, but several official looking persons boarded the train. After about twenty minutes we were asked to re-board the train to continue our journey. I asked the ticket inspector what it was all about, and he said that a box of serviettes had been left on the counter by one of the staff.

So wasn't Lilian lucky to get her handbag back!

The rest of the journey home went without incident, friend Colin Emsley picked us up in his car and took us to our door.

Thank you, Margaret and Jersey.

# Chapter 10

## *Blind Date* - Behind the screen

A special show was put on by LWT to celebrate the first ten years of *Blind Date*, to show some of the highlights, and to explain some of the mysteries that go on backstage.

If by chance you watched this show, and I sincerely hope that you did, you would have had some idea of the magnitude of the work involved in the production of each year's series of shows: of the auditioning of approximately eleven thousand applicants across the country, and of the whittling down to about one hundred and sixty whom the producers would consider as suitable to appear on this very popular show.

As one-time contestants, Lilian and I were pleased to see the *behind the screen* bit, showing what goes on during the actual performance of the show, as we have been right through the process and have come out smiling at the end. We had reached the highest goal of all, and, let's face it, isn't the ultimate aim of any dating process, be it *on the box*, through a newspaper or any other medium, to match together two people who will eventually fall in love with each other?

Those who present themselves at an audition do so for many reasons, perhaps best known to themselves. These reasons I have no doubt are conveyed to the researchers, after all, there is no point in any interview unless the character and feelings of the interviewee are placed on the table, to enable some assessment to be made. What salient points are looked for by the panel, I am not qualified to say, neither would I presume that I could in any way match the expertise of those with whom the responsibility of maintaining the popularity of the show rests.

From Lilian's and my points of view, and after all, that what this book is all about, we have the highest praise for all with whom we came into contact, and why shouldn't we? Look at what has happened to us, two ordinary people who met together under these quite unusual circumstances, one from the North, one from the South of England, going through the auditions, hoping for selection because we wanted to enjoy ourselves along with others with a similar viewpoint. What a splendid opportunity if we could beat the odds and get through to the finals, a challenge indeed. Let's have a go!

We decided to write this book for several reasons. So far as we are aware it has not been done before, we have something to write about that is unique, it may be of interest to anybody contemplating auditioning for the next series, incidentally don't be deterred by anything I may have written that will give you the collywobbles, it's a fascinating experience, believe me. To get back to the reasons for this book, because what I am writing about occurred just recently, and all over just a very short period of time, if we don't do it now, we never will. If we let the opportunity slip away, we will be letting ourselves down. If you have been on any of the shows, I hope this will bring back some of the memories.

There is one very important reason for this book: Lilian and I wanted to convey to all the readers, viewers and potential viewers, our appreciation for all the affection and friendship, and love as well, that has come to us from all sources. If we didn't tell you, how would you know how much we appreciate and try to return that affection? If the critics say what a load of drivel, I don't care, I want to get my message across.

This book is also a tribute to all of you who give us a smile as you pass us in the street, a word of congratulation, a handshake or an autograph. And to the estimated two thousand of you who stood outside Tiverton Registry Office, some I understand for four hours, on that cold February day to cheer and wave, (didn't Lilian look lovely in her cream suit?) you all helped, and are still helping to make our togetherness complete.

To return to the theme of this chapter, from which I have somewhat digressed (call it author's licence) Lilian and I had received an invitation via Nina to appear on this centenary show, made in November for screening in December.

We duly presented ourselves in the studio and met our friends who were involved in the production, plus other contestants who had also been invited to participate.

We met for the first time, Alex and Sue Tatham. Their's was the first Blind Date wedding, and we learnt that Alex used to do Tarzanograms, and Sue Kissograms. I was the odd one out here, because Lilian also did Kissograms. What had I been missing? Alex and Sue also had with them their baby Emily, we can remember reading about the birth of baby Emily on the daily news board of the Canberra whilst we were on that cruise. There was Paul from Tyne and Wear, now running a disco, and used to be a window cleaner, and does a good impression of Bruce Forsyth, and did one on the show. Great! Claudia, a great personality, sings in the London clubs, and will always be remembered for her great part when she appeared. Tina from Liverpool who worked in a fish shop, and told Cilla that she still does. Elaine, a talented singer. I could go on, there were many, who, over the years had brought so much fun and entertainment to the viewers. I must mention Paul who appeared on the very first show, he told us that whilst on his *date* all the photographs taken were stills, a sign of the times, because now a whole crew goes with the couple. In all it was a very good representation of some of the favourite moments chosen from a decade.

There were highlights from the two weddings, both of which, due to the very nature of them, had attracted so much attention, and captured the hearts of so many.

I feel privileged, Cilla, in that I can talk to you through the medium of this book, and I am sure that you must be proud of your achievement over the past ten years, and in respect of the enjoyment you have created through the *Blind Date* show for many millions of people, and that you and your team have been able to continue the momentum which is so necessary in this great project. In our specific case, you have been the cause of making two of your fans extremely happy.

We both loved this show, the bits about Ted Robbins chatting to the audience, seeing and meeting Graham, our *voice*, even seeing the operator winding back that partition, referred to countless times as *when the screen went back*; will somebody one day say *when the barrier receded* or something akin to that?

Cilla referred to the seat on which sat the picker as being the hottest seat on the show; well I suppose it is really, considering the dilemma which the occupant must be faced with. I tried to imagine myself in Lilian's position, what would have swayed me to choose One, Two or Three? There's not much time to create a mental picture built up from the answers, perhaps some little quirk rings a bell in the brain, triggered off by our Graham's summing up. Lilian said that it was my voice that decided her, well, so be it. Had I not been told this, I would have assumed that she tossed an invisible coin, heads for Number One, tails for Number Three, and, hold it, safety in the middle Number Two. Or it could have been the invisible friend who jumped up and down in her chair shouting 'pick Number Two!' who tapped into Lilian's brain circuit? If she did, I thank her.

Come to think of it, When Alex Tatham picked Sue as his date, she was also a Number Two. Could there be any significance in that?

This most exclusive club in Britain, to which Alex referred and welcomed us to in his message to us on our wedding day, and in which he said that we had just doubled the membership, could be named *The Number Two Club*. But on reflection that might be an omen which could deter later would-be marriage partners from membership of this exclusive club. It would have to be *Cilla's Blind Date Wedding Club*. Now come on you lot, there are sufficient members for a President, Chairman, Secretary and Vice Chairman, but where are the other members? Don't mess about, we'll soon be calling an AGM, and we need the support. The only fees are a commitment for life.

Seriously, though, baby Emily stole the show. We liked the part when Cilla was holding her, and when passing her back to her mum she said, 'Now I know how Lady Thatcher feels.'

Cilla also said that maybe we would all meet again on the twentieth anniversary, now that's food for thought. I only hope that Lilian and I can make it: I'll try, even if they have to dig me up for this one. Now that would be a challenge for the make-up department, wouldn't it?

In ten years the advancement in technology of television, although unpredictable from the layman's point of view, could mean that three-dimensional television would come to our screens, and we will be stepping off those stools (by the way, they are the second hottest seats on the show, at least mine felt like it to the touch) right into the viewers' lounge: 'No sugar or milk in mine, please'.

After the show we were invited up to the hospitality room for a glass or two of wine, and to be with Cilla when she cut her cake.

The hospitality room is high up in the London Television Centre building, and has a large window, from which one has a panoramic view of London, particularly beautiful at night. It is a view that we both are accustomed to admiring, the memory of which we take away with us each time after our visit.

There were party balloons with the *Blind Date* logo, two of which my dear wife managed to salvage and take with us. They made one little lad happy when Lilian gave them to him on the train back to Devon, the next morning.

# Chapter 11

## Our First Anniversary

Before I come to the celebrations and events of this anniversary, I would like to go back over the year, to portray some of the highlights and moments of special significance which we have been privileged to experience.

During these twelve months we travelled extensively, by train, road and air, although so far not by hot air balloon or army tank. We have stayed in many hotels, eaten countless meals in restaurants (have you ever eaten fish and chips in Chez Fred's in Bournemouth? If not, try it!) Above all we have been given the opportunity to meet so many people, and make so many good friends.

From the day of our wedding, every event fell into place, as if the whole sequence had been carefully planned from the start: the honeymoon, followed by the fishing weekend, then the cruise on the Canberra, the Battle of Flowers in Jersey, the fêtes and the shop openings, interspersed by holidays in Bournemouth as guests of our friend Margaret, with whom we also spent the New Year's celebrations. I can with absolute certainty say that *That was the year that was.*

To proceed with the anniversary, before the day arrived, things began to hot up. The telephone rang repeatedly, West Country Television sent along a reporter and photographer, resulting in an interview and pictures of us at the local Church, the scene of our Blessing. They also requested we attend their local studio to do a live interview on the Friday before the anniversary. The same day a reporter and photographer from *The Daily Mirror* arrived for a story, and they wished us to be photographed with the Jersey Potteries clock. Now this one was the second clock, given to us that we may raffle it and donate the proceeds to charity. *The Daily Mirror* had agreed to do a *phone-in* draw for this beautifully made timepiece, a dead ringer for the one which hangs on our lounge wall, signed by Cilla and ourselves before firing. Subsequently a picture of the two of us holding the clock appeared in the *Mirror Woman* section along with a full page feature entitled *Our Blind Date Love is never going to die,* very nicely written by Janie Lawrence. We learnt later that the clock had been won by a lady living in the Midlands. The proceeds went to the British Heart Foundation.

Chris telephoned from London Weekend Television to tell us that he had been asked if we would be willing to appear on *The Crystal Rose Show*, for Carlton Television. This would be in the London studio, two days after our anniversary. We were pleased to accept, contacted by Asif, on behalf of the television company, who kindly arranged for our transport and accommodation over night.

Tony Hardman asked if we would formally open a Wedding Exhibition at the Bournemouth International Centre on Friday the third of February. Things were going to be a bit tight, we didn't want to double book, it's not nice to let people down. One thing I have found to be one hundred per cent necessary is to have a large diary, to have it to hand when the telephone rings, and to record all the relevant material immediately, plus a telephone number to ring back in case of any query. I learned this in my business training way back, but I must admit I didn't expect to have to do it when I retired. Oops! I must write in *don't forget the anniversary card for Lilian*. Number one priority, never forget the wife's birthday or anniversary card, never mind the present, it's the thought that counts! Wallop! Ouch! Sorry dear, I didn't mean it, here's a little something to put matters right!

We had been in Bournemouth having another holiday with Margaret, returning home on January 31st. It now meant a return journey on the quick, but never mind, it's all part of the fun.

We had made arrangements for a couple of days away on our own for the anniversary, around which we fitted the commitments we had made. So off we went back to Bournemouth, where Tony had made arrangements for us to stay at the Bournemouth International Hotel for the night preceding the show. A large four-poster bed and a private jacuzzi were luxuries we enjoyed whilst at this hotel. The jacuzzi was large enough for four, but we settled for just the two of us. What fun! An evening meal, a good night's rest and we were ready to go, but first a good lunch with Tony and off to our dressing room to prepare. We had thought that it would be a fitting gesture if we opened the exhibition whilst wearing the same clothes which we had worn on our wedding day. Mind you, we both had to breathe in deeply to enable the zips and buttons to engage properly. 'These trousers have shrunk about two inches around the waist, dear.' But success came in the end.

Upon entering the exhibition area, we were introduced. Lilian was presented with a large basket of flowers, and after a few words we cut the tape, declaring the exhibition formally open. There followed a very interesting tour around the stands, which covered every imaginable requirement for the wedding arrangements. There is no point in my listing them, but you name it, it was there. All the memories came flooding back as we toured. We met one young lady working on a stand whom we had previously met in the hospitality room of the studio when we were on the *Blind Date* show. What a small world we live in!

But then of course, Cilla's show is very popular and has been going for ten years. Lots have attended the auditions, not so many have got on the shows, but still a considerable number, and it is the kind of experience that can never be forgotten, it leaves an indelible impression behind. We have always been happy to talk to those who have trod the same path, and will continue to do so. If you have not attended an audition, and considered that you wanted to, that you had what it takes, but needed that little push in the right direction, heed my words, go for it! I had my little push, quite a big push in fact, but just look at my prize! No, I am not on a commission from LWT on the number of recruits that I may raise, do it for your own self, for your enjoyment and your own sense of achievement.

It is astonishing the number of businesses and personnel who are engaged solely in the business of marriage, whose purpose is to contribute some part in the whole sequence of the ceremony. I personally feel that it is a shame that the popularity of a proper wedding with all the frills has dwindled in this modern age. Couldn't we bring back the days when every young or elderly couple wanted to have their day of happy remembrance? What is needed to re-kindle the spirit and the thrill? Sadly I do not have the answer to that one. Is it anything to do with this *feel good factor* or *going back to basics* or both?

I know that I feel proud to introduce Lilian as my wife, the lady I love: although in fact in our particular case it is seldom necessary, as we were told that over ten million viewers watched our wedding on their television screens, but nevertheless you will know what I mean.

Leaving the exhibition and Bournemouth at around three o'clock, we headed for Taunton and our West Country television appointment. The weather was atrocious, wind, driving rain, dark and foggy, on top of which I took a wrong turning and was heading in the wrong direction. But we made it with time to spare before going on the air. After the television interview Lilian was given a bouquet of flowers, and a bottle of bubbly for me, with the compliments of West Country Television, to celebrate our anniversary. Thank you!

Upon our arrival home, another bouquet of flowers was waiting for us, this time from the London Weekend Television team members, and it had been taken in by our kind neighbour.

On Saturday morning, the eve of the anniversary, more flowers arrived, a large bouquet from Cilla and Bobby, another from Margaret. The door bell and the telephone rang constantly while we were attempting to pack for our weekend away.

A reporter from *The Sun* newspaper rang for a telephone interview, telling us that a photographer was on his way. He arrived shortly after, and, seeing all the flowers, decided that a shot taken with us surrounded by the flowers would look good. What he didn't know was that we had run short of vases. Lilian had come up with the solution: large empty coffee jars disguised with fancy paper and ribbon which, when she had arranged them all, fitted in very nicely. I'll say this for Lilian, when it comes to bright ideas for situations like that, she's no slouch! There followed a walk to the church to snap us feeding the ducks with a bread roll he had purchased from the Grocer's shop, which reminded us that we hadn't had lunch, time was running short, and we had over a hundred miles to drive.

We had booked a double room at the Seymour House Hotel, Chipping Campden, in the Cotswolds, through Classic Breakaway. They had assured us we had made an excellent choice, and they were not wrong. We were not disappointed, far from it. When we arrived we were told that we had been upgraded to a suite, and it was indeed very, very comfortable and exquisitely furnished. We then took a short walk along the main street to admire the many antique and gift shops before returning for an evening meal with a good wine to complete the day.

Sunday February 5th 1995, precisely one year of marriage was now under our belts, so to speak, and we had confounded the critics, oh yes! We have had only a few, and one rumour which we heard started in a hairdresser's shop in Newcastle, that we were having a divorce! A divorce? Not on your nelly! It's amazing how a rumour will spread from a casual word spoken, without foundation. Well it got back to us, and we just laughed, let them have their little bit of fun and speculation, we know the truth, they'll have red faces when they read this book.

We drove into the nearby district of Broadway, again full of antique and gift shops, and cosy little olde worlde tea shops, where we had our lunch. We spoke to many well-wishers, told them it was our anniversary, and congratulations were the order of the day. Although it was February, many people, like us, were popping in and out of these charming shops, what a fascinating part of the country we were in.

Back to the hotel for our anniversary meal, with a bottle of champagne to celebrate. And, do you know, the telephone didn't ring once!

Not so the next day when we arrived home. The answering machine was full of messages. We understood from some of our callers that day that they were unable to get through to the machine because the tape was full. Most of the messages were those congratulating us, then we had two local papers who wanted some information for their editorials, eventually resulting in another photographer's visit, and more pictures with the flowers.

Come Tuesday, we were off again by train to London, to the Carlton Television studio for *The Crystal Rose Show*. Upon arrival in reception we were very glad to meet some of our friends employed on the *Blind Date* show, who were in the same building, so it was hugs and kisses all round. It wasn't unusual, I believe most if not all of the staff knew us by now. I suppose we are very lucky in many respects: when we go shopping, and, unlike most husbands, I like shopping, we don't necessarily get preferential treatment which would be unfair, but so many times we get that extra smile, and 'How are you both?' and 'How's Cilla?'

On to the show, the theme being *Love*, a subject which we believed was not alien to us, and they liked our story. It was a very entertaining show, the live audience was packed. I feel sure that everybody enjoyed it as much as Lilian and I did. A novel way was used to identify those whom had been selected to be spoken to by Crystal: a heart-shaped balloon was fixed to the backs of their seats. I must admit to one disappointment, due to the pressure of the past few days, I had omitted to programme my video, so did not have a copy of this particular show. I usually video any show on which we have appeared, for record purposes. My loss, my fault.

It was at this show that we met Stewart Ferris, who, I may say, had been named by Company Magazine as one of the country's top fifty eligible bachelors. How about that, girls? And we've since met his mum too, and to coin a phrase which we have been hearing of late, *she's a bit of alright!*

Hmm! Well, meeting Stewart and discussing with him the possibilities of a book of our experiences, it was this chance meeting that finally decided the go-ahead on this book. How many of us have said at one time or another *I could write a book*, and the thought has then been tossed aside? My only previous writings have been those of a technical nature when a long time ago I was employed by Consulting Engineers to rummage through the records of ships, in the archives of Lloyds Register of Shipping, to determine the history of the vessel in question in order to satisfy a potential buyer of its suitability for purchase. To venture into the field of writing, I consider, requires first that it be a subject of common interest, that it captures the imagination, has a hint of humour, hurts no one, and in the case of this book, has messages of love. It is necessary to have a dedication to the creation of the work. To embark on the project requires support and guidance, and I thank Stewart for both of these. So the fruits of this meeting have clinched the deal that we now have.

What a super first anniversary for Lilian and myself.

# Chapter 12

## August 1995 - Return to Jersey

Our last visit to the Island of Jersey was as guests of Margaret Beadle, to last year's Battle of Flowers parade. Again, this year, Margaret, Vice President of the Battle Association, had invited Lilian and I as her guests, to participate once more in this glorious extravaganza. The invitation gladdened our hearts, and was one which we were overjoyed to accept.

The concept of the Battle of Flowers was first born, when, in 1902, the Coronation of King Edward VII and Queen Alexandra was celebrated in Jersey, with island-wide participation in a floral festival along Victoria Avenue, which lies parallel to the sea front. Within a few minutes of the finish of the parade spectators and participants used flowers from the displays to bombard each other. The festival was considered to be a great success, and was the start of an annual tradition, a tradition which was carried on until the outbreak of the first World War in 1914, when it was suspended.

In 1938 the Battle was re-introduced, the parade being held in a Stadium, a football and cattle show ground just on the outskirts of St. Helier. The outbreak of World War II in 1939, however, once again caused the Battle of Flowers to be halted.

In 1951 the floral tradition was once again re-introduced, when, as we understood, it was forecast that the revival would boost the island's tourist trade. The forty thousand spectators confirmed the popularity and its success.

The following year, 1952, marked the 50th anniversary of the event, when it once again attained Royal significance, the Golden Jubilee coinciding with the accession of Queen Elizabeth II.

The first Miss Battle was elected in 1953, and following that, a competition is held every year from all twelve parishes, competing for the 'Miss Battle' crown. The year after, the Miss Battle was accompanied by a celebrity taking the title of 'Mr Battle'. This feature is now an established part of the 'Battle of Flowers'. Unlike the horse-drawn carriages and bicycles of yester-year, the modern floats are mostly motorised, although we did notice that some of them are still pushed or pulled by hand. We were intrigued to know that some of the drivers of these floats were deep down in the bowels of the exhibits, and guided by walkie talkie or some other electronic device, either that or they peered through some unobtrusive slit in some part of the huge displays.

We were told that there was a size limit to the displays, in the region of some forty five feet long and sixteen feet high. The limits existed due to the difficulties of manoeuvring round the corners, along the roads and under the trees.

Incidentally, I did come across some trimming of the trees along the roadside, no doubt for that purpose. On another occasion during the days before the parade, I happened to be driving through St. Brelades following a lorry which had a lifting device on the back, the upper extremity of which, I believe quite unknown to the driver, was doing its own tree trimming, scattering leaves and small branches in its wake. I must admit to leaving a sizeable gap between us as we followed, it was a bit like travelling behind a hay lorry which is moving at speed, but much worse.

During the fifties and early sixties the traditional throwing of flowers was retained, until 1964, when the organisers decided, for safety  reasons, that the 'Battle' should cease-fire, and that the finale should take on a different form. 'Petals from Heaven', masses of strips of coloured paper were dropped from an aircraft, but a whole bag of these was apparently pushed out by accident, falling perilously close to spectators below, so this idea was abandoned. Every year now the finale takes on a different form.

My brain was in gear, and must have got jammed: here's me going on about the past, I hadn't yet arrived in Jersey. Having driven to Weymouth, my car and its two passengers booked on the Condor 11, joined the queue of cars awaiting embarkation. The ferry was late in arriving, and when the sleek twin-hulled vessel approached, I heard one small lad say, 'Dad, it's got a hole in it.' Fortunately it was in its designed place, or we might have changed our minds about boarding. I do hope 'Dad' put his lad's mind at rest, or the poor little chap might have spent the whole voyage feverishly counting his chances of survival, one eye on his tin of cola and the other on his lifebelt beneath the seat.

When I drove on board, I was guided to the upper deck, halted three inches from the car beside me, and had to get out of the car by clambering across the seats to the passenger side, not an easy task considering the cockpit type arrangement in the front of a Mondeo, and the fault of two knees which would only bend in one direction. But, all that aside, we were safely on board. The weather was fine and we had a great trip. It wasn't so good for a few, though, and one little grey faced lad sat with his head immersed in a bag, so we gave his Dad an anti-sickness pill for him, which calmed him, and he spent the rest of the voyage curled up asleep. Believe me, I knew how he felt: four years in the Navy, mostly at sea, and we had no remedy for sea-sickness in those days. I had spent many hours with my stomach in my mouth. Horrible thought!

We had quite a few conversations with fellow passengers, some of whom asked 'Weren't you on *Blind Date*?', which usually followed with 'Are you still happily married?' Sometimes it was 'You both look better in real life than you do on the televison!' or 'So you are going back to Jersey again!' What marvellous memories people have, it is now eighteen months since we married. I firmly suspect that if Lilian took the bow out of her hair, and I shaved off my beard, that nobody would recognise us. But for what reason would we wish to do that? We are quite happy to stop and talk, and even if we did both of those things, and we walked through the streets of New York, somebody would stop us and say 'Excuse me, were you on *Blind Date*?' Such is the embracing power of Television and the Press.

I can assure anybody whose interest is such, that it is not embarrassing, far from it, it is lovely to be greeted with a smile and a word of friendliness.

We were greeted with a smile when we landed, Margaret's daughter-in-law Vicki waved to us and signalled to us to follow her to Margaret's home in St Brelades.

As we were over an hour later than our anticipated time of arrival, evening dinner arrangements had to be changed. So we dined with Margaret at the Bistro Soleil. Afterwards we drove over to meet with Buster Merryfield and his wife Iris at the Hotel where they were staying for the duration of the 'Battle', being also guests of Margaret. That night, by arrangement, we were guests at Margaret's home.

The following morning, Saturday, we drove to the Battle of Flowers Association fête. The weather was very hot, and a perfect day for a fête. John Inman, who was currently appearing in a show *Fancy Free* at the Jersey Opera House, officially opened the event, and as he passed us on his way to the dais he said 'Hello' and gave us a smile. Buster sat on the dais. There were presentations of flowers and wine, then Lilian and I were asked to appear on the dais to be presented to the assembled spectators.

We were invited to try a 'Wonder of Jersey' by a couple with a stall, which was a tasty doughnut with a twist, made on the spot. Very nice and moreish. We had lunch on the lawn, watched the tug-o-war stalwarts digging in their heels and pulling for all they were worth. Girls were also in the teams. It was all too energetic for me, just watching was exhausting enough. The winners were presented with a trophy by Margaret. There was a lot to see, including a demonstration of martial arts, breaking of tiles by the hand and by the head, plus breaking a block of concrete on a fellow's chest with a sledgehammer. A brilliant display by a team of Majorettes in perfect timing was also given.

The evening was rounded off by dinner at the Chateau Valeuse Hotel, St. Brelades, where we were guests of the Battle of Flowers committee.

Sunday saw us all at the Jersey Flower Centre, where we also met Buster's daughter Karen and son-in-law Rodney who were holidaying in Jersey also at Margaret's invitation. Lunch was served in the open, and the Bridgtown Band played some very rousing tunes and kept everybody amused, especially when the three trombonists appeared on a balcony and joined in the music with a swing. There were a number of loud bangs, and up in the air shot loads of paper and silk flowers and confetti, fluttering down, descending on all of us like snow.

At the antique car show we wandered around admiring the care and workmanship of restoration which the owners had lovingly carried out. After departing, it was to the Chateau de la Mer for coffee, then on to the sea front, where there was being held in the bay a competition for the best decorated yacht. Johnny Day, comedian, was present at the beach side, and greeted us when we arrived. He was compering the beach activities, which included another tug-o-war, the winner of which received a prize from Margaret.

On the Monday, after lunch, the five of us, Margaret, Buster, Iris, Lilian and myself, wearing our Judge's badges, had the allotted task of visiting in turn the shops who had entered the competition for the best decorated Floral window display. We had the same task last year, and were very pleased to be asked to do it once again. The standard was high, and after completing the rounds, we conferred and made our selection for the winners.

Came the evening, we attended *The Minstrels* show at Swansons on the Esplanade, a very lively show with singers and dancers, and including Stevie Bee, comedian, and Olaf Blakeley with his magic show. Speaking with Olaf later, he did tell me that he had thought of inviting me on to the stage to assist in his act with the 'magic rings' and put my head in his guillotine, but he thought that it might embarrass me. Pity, it would have been an experience, but there again, things do sometimes go wrong, and I needed my clear head to carry on with my writing.

Tuesday morning we decided to visit some of our friends in St. Aubin, Bill and Olive Fleuret in their gift shop, then to Adrian in his Matisse beauty salon. Then on to Colette in her cabin on the sea front, where last year we judged the children's sand castles on the beach. Colette and her husband were pleased to see us again. We had our lunch there before making our way back to prepare for our next official engagement.

This was for a live broadcast interview with Murray Norton, on BBC Radio Jersey and Guernsey, at 3.00 p.m. At the appointed time we arrived at the Grand

Hotel, the interview being held on the front terrace. It was very hot, and there was a lot of traffic passing by, but for us it was a happy occasion to answer the questions that Murray put to us, principally on our lives since our marriage. It was also an opportune moment to speak on the air about the launching of this book. Buster also had a long talk, and Margaret spoke about the forthcoming Battle parade.

We noticed that whilst we were chatting with Murray, live on the radio, a number of cars passing by were sounding their horns, and we realised that they had their car radios tuned in on the station, and were listening to us as they drove past. I am sure that it was one of the longest live radio interviews that Lilian and I had spoken on. Chatting to Murray after coming off the air, he explained that he himself had been a contestant on one of Cilla Black's *Blind Date* shows, some time back, and that he had been picked by a very tall blonde lady, and they went on a date to Brands Hatch. In his case, however, he said that there had been no chemistry between them, and there was no follow up after the date. Nevertheless, it was an interesting story, and as I had stated before, we had always been glad to hear of others' experiences.

That evening we went back into St Helier to witness an organised bedpush. I must admit to being a little confused as to whether it had been a race or a parade, but whatever, it caused a great deal of fun and laughter, with many young children taking part. One ancient basket-like bed with large wire wheels, bedecked with balloons and with a very brave volunteer as a passenger, or patient, or victim, appeared to be from the Victorian era. Another, weighted down with lots of children on it, had to discharge its cargo of kids as it almost caved in, and the wheels buckled up under the strain. The police were marvellous in controlling the traffic to make way for the beds and the pushers. They appeared to be careering in all directions, much like supermarket trolleys.

After driving around, we finally came on what appeared to be the finish of the 'push', and the police were assisting by putting the beds into their van, before returning them to their owners.

Wednesday, the eve of the 'Battle' was spent by Lilian and I shopping in St. Helier. It's a great shopping area, and one which we always make the effort to visit when we are on the island.

The Town Hall was our next engagement, the 'Vin de Honeur' when the trophies for floral decorations of shops, hotels, guest houses, pubs and races etc. were presented to the winners of these events. The constable's wife gave us liberation lapel badges, which, we understood later were not easy to come by, the comments being 'where did you get your badges?'

It was at this function in the Town Hall where Lionel Blair arrived, as the following day he was due to act as the 'Mr Battle'. He told me that he would be reading this book: thanks, Lionel, I hope you are not disappointed.

We made a visit to some of the float building sheds, where all were busy with the last touches of fixing on the fresh flowers, each one being individually trimmed and glued in place, many thousands of them. We saw that it was a last minute job, to apply them while they were fresh, especially during this very hot spell of weather. As I had explained during our last year's visit, such dedication and hard work by all the helpers had to be admired.

Thursday, Battle Day, arrived. The traffic was re-routed around town, so we went in by taxi. First to the marquee behind the VIP stand, for lunch, after which we took up our seats, which were located in the front row of the stand almost opposite the VIP enclosure. From these seats we had a magnificent view of all the parade that went by.

It was a good position to take pictures, and fortunately I had a camcorder with me, and was able to get some good footage of the show. And so the cavalcade of floats, dancers, bands, majorettes etc passed by, up one side of the dual road, and down the other, in what seemed to be a never ending procession of sound, colour and magical display. I could not describe the floats so that it would do them justice, it really had to be seen to be appreciated. One or two of the larger floats sprang to my mind, the *Memphis Belle*, the *Spooky Train* the *Hocus Pocus* and the *Valley of the Kings*. There was one of the smaller floats which had been designed by a seven year old lad, which he called *Yabadabadoo* (I hope I've spelt it correctly). His ambition is to be in on one of the large ones. He had started young, but such appeared to be the tradition and the spirit for now and the future. Good luck!

Fortunately we had purchased hats, as advised, the sun beat down on us, but no one could have asked for better conditions. Confetti flew everywhere, and a number of the float passengers were throwing real flowers into the assembled crowds. Lionel Blair was up on top of the float along with Miss Battle and her Maids, all of them waving and joining in the fun along with the crowds.

When the procession had finally completed the circuit, we had made our way back to the marquee for a welcome cup of tea before departing. But the day was not over, we returned again that evening, this time we had seats in the enclosure, to witness the Band parade.

The Bournemouth Scout and Guide Band, The Ostre Baerum Promenadeorkester from Norway, the Bridgtown Concert Show Band, and the Romsey Old Cadet Carnival Show Band. All of these, plus the Band of the Island of Jersey all gave great performances. Soon after the show started, Lionel, who was in the centre of the front row of the enclosure, stood up and swayed and moved his body, arms and legs to the rhythm of the music.

We had then noticed a young lad, high up in the stand which was on the opposite side of the road, was following and repeating all of Lionel's movements. It was great to see them both, the lad following his every movement. It was a fine double act, and the crowd loved it. It was getting dark, and Lionel gave him one of those fluorescent torches, and sent it over via the vendor.

The Romsey Old Cadet Band were all dressed up as gnomes, and when one of them exploded some kind of banger, they all collapsed headlong on the ground. After the last band of the evening, the Jersey Band, completed and marched off to the applause of the people, Lionel met up with his fellow performer, Lee, aged about twelve, and congratulated him.

I am sure that everybody agreed that the bands were great, but the success of that evening, the stars, belonged to Lionel and Lee. Congratulations to you both for such a great performance, and I am sure that I speak for all assembled there that evening when I say thanks to you.

Friday morning we were taken to the grounds where the floats were assembled, some of which were having their lighting fitted in readiness for the Moonlight Parade. On some of the units the lighting had been incorporated during the initial building. On the others the bulbs etc were installed later. It was an occasion where the public could view the entries at close quarters. There were also in the grounds various stalls where mementos and gifts could be purchased. Lilian was in her glory here, searching for things to take back home for the family.

As guests again of Margaret we arrived at La Haule Manor, with Lionel, Buster, Iris and her family, and together with other guests of Margaret we had another great meal prior to watching the Moonlight Parade. Margaret and Lionel had set off early, in order to get to the start, and the traffic situation being seen as a problem, with Margaret's ingenuity she obtained the help of the police to assist their journey. After the meal we had to drive in to park our cars, and inch by inch eventually arrived at the car park, and took up our seats in the VIP enclosure. Another glorious show lit up by the thousands of lights on the floats as they passed slowly before us. Miss Battle and Lionel once more waved to the crowds. It was late when finally the show came to the end, another very satisfying and colourful event.

Saturday, we left the flatlet where we had been staying, and returned to Margaret's home. That evening, similar to last year, we spent in the Hotel de France, and was the occasion for the Battle of Flowers Association exhibitors' presentation evening. After the meal and the speeches, the winners were called up to receive their trophies, to much cheering, one could see that they were most coveted awards. The Jersey Accordion band and the Bridgtown band played to the guests, there was much singing and the cracking of party poppers. The party went with a bang, a disco took over and there was dancing to the early hours. At one thirty in the morning we had called it a day and departed. Sleep, oh glorious sleep!

Sunday morning, Buster's Daughter and her husband departed for the ferry and home. Then in the evening we accompanied Buster and Iris to the Airport, to see them off on their flight home.

Monday, Margaret accompanied us to the ferry terminal, and so back on the Condor 11 we left for the mainland and home. It was goodbye to Jersey once again, and to a wonderful holiday. Our thanks to Margaret for everything. As we passed Portelet Bay, through binoculars we saw Margaret in her garden, waving a white sheet to wish us *bon voyage*.

Jersey, the Honeymoon Island? You bet it is.

# Chapter 13

## The Ongoing Year and the Future

Most of the significant exciting things which happened to the two of us are outlined in the preceding chapters, all of which in no possible way could we have predicted. Two ordinary people, living hundreds of miles apart, coming together, experiencing so much in such a short space of time.

The fact that we both had reached the *three score years and ten* stage made it even more remarkable. But in no way is that the end of the story, obscurity only happens if you let it, and that's not on our agenda. So long as we are both able, we will continue to get the interest out of life, and planning for the future in so much as we are able, but also living in the present.

As well as being a summing-up of the whole period of our short lives together, I am about to describe some of the additional events which occurred from time to time, not covered in the previous chapters.

Nevertheless they all form part of the memories of our relationship.

They can all be classed under the heading of humorous events, as without exception they raise a chuckle each time we recall and talk of them.

For example, I have already mentioned my feelings when I approached the Registry Office in Tiverton on the day of the wedding, when I saw all the barriers, and thought the road was up, and that we might have difficulty in getting through. It wasn't until we got near to the Town Hall that I realised that all those people were there to see the wedding. About a week after our return from honeymoon we returned to Tiverton, to be greeted by many as we walked through the town, The Chief of Police spotted us from across the road, came over to shake our hands, and with a grin said, 'You are not giving me so much trouble as the last time you were here.' But he also told us that he had had a very nice letter from London Weekend Television. I have no doubt that it would have been thanking the police for their part in the proceedings. It was some months later, also in Tiverton, that we were speaking to a young man who introduced himself as John, saying that he had joined the Special Constabulary, and his very first assignment was at our wedding. He also said that somebody had murmured in the crowd about the cost of policing the wedding, and the Chief turned to John and said to him, 'Tell them why you are here.'

'I volunteered, like the rest of us,' replied John.

There have been many instances that spring to mind. A friend of mine had told me that he was once stopped in the street by a lady who asked for his autograph, but she didn't have a piece of paper to write it on, and suggested he sign on her leg, which he refused. Whereupon she pursued him, fished a dirty piece of paper out of the gutter, possibly an old till receipt, and suggested he write on this!

I haven't had an experience quite like that, but on one occasion, Lilian and I were looking in a shop window, and we noticed two young girls, aged about ten or eleven standing beside us, looking in the same window. We moved on to look in another shop, and there they were again, right beside us. By this time we had reached the Electricity Board show room, and went inside to look at some fridge-freezers, and yes, there they were still beside us. This was no coincidence, so Lilian said, 'Hullo,' to which one girl replied, 'We saw you on *Blind Date*.' Lilian asked them if they were wanting our autograph, the answer being, 'Yes, please!' They had no paper, neither did we. Not to be beaten by this temporary lack of writing material, I took the bold step of asking the young lady sitting at her desk if she could provide the necessary scrap of paper in order that we might make these two young fans of ours happy.

'Only these,' she said, taking a couple of product literature pamphlets from the wall rack. Well, that was fine, and the task completed, we were about to resume our fridge quest when a lady dashed out of the room, to return with, we assumed, her granddaughter, who, breathless, came over to us and gasped out, 'My name's Jane, can I have one too, please?'

Then one of the first two girls returned saying, 'Can I have one for my Grandma, please, because she loves you?'

By this time the shop manager had arrived to see what was going on, possibly wondering how so many pamphlets on one product were going out in such a short time, and then he laughed and said, 'Oh! It's you.'

The signing of autographs had been a new experience for us, although not an enthusiastic autograph hunter myself, nevertheless I had always imagined this sort of thing was only associated with football or cricket or tennis players and the like, and people of prominence in the entertainment field. However, I must say that I enjoy this new found side of our lives: the smiles of recognition, the handshakes, the whispered congratulations. I am sure that Lilian and I both think that this was not really happening, and in consequence view the situation with a certain amount of awe.

I recall us walking through the centre of Liverpool when in front of us appeared a lady of more than ample proportions pushing a shopper bag, which she dropped, her eyes opened wide, and with a beaming smile and a booming voice she clasped us to her ample bosom in one mighty swoop. When we came up for air we shook hands and one happy lady went on her way.

We were sitting on a bench in Tiverton, a lady stopped, told us that she had been on the canal side, and a local artist whom she knew said that some children had been calling after him, 'Hullo, David Fensom!' and 'Who is he?'

She told him that the children were confusing him with me, as we were *look-alikes*.

On our way to the car park we noticed a lady with a gentleman talking by the roadside, recognised him at once, and asked him if his name was Dudley, to which he replied, 'Not if I owe you money,' an answer after my own heart! So the three of us sat on a bench, had a little chat and, having my camera with me, took some pics of him with Lilian, and the two of us together. Now wasn't that an unusual coincidence!

Tolerance of people one to another we have found in the West Country to be very high. It was now seven years since I had *emigrated* from the east side of Britain, and just over one year for Lilian from the north east, and we seem to have settled with no problems, and what's more, we feel that we are accepted, which is important for our peace of mind.

We were just finishing a midday meal in a department store restaurant in Taunton when a couple who had been sitting at an adjoining table came over and asked if we would mind if we had our photograph taken with them. Whereupon all the crockery and cutlery disappeared off our table, all the chairs were re-arranged and somebody snapped the four of us together. Then the crockery etc was replaced, and all carried on as if nothing had happened. Things have more or less normalised in our local towns now, those who know us still smile and say, 'Hullo,' or, 'How are you?' Sometimes it's, 'Saw you on the television,' or, 'You were in the newspaper again.'

As Lilian's daughter Linda and her family live in Liverpool, quite naturally we spend some time with them. Incidentally Linda does voluntary work with ARC, (Appeal for Rumanian Children), and has visited Rumania in conjunction with this work. During one of our visits we noticed that *Blind Date* were holding first auditions in a local hotel, so we decided to pop in and give them a surprise. As we walked to the hotel a car stopped alongside us, and out came Samantha, a college student who had been on the same show as us. We meet them everywhere! Upon arrival at the hotel, we proceeded to the waiting room where the contestants had gathered. At the moment of our arrival they were chanting the *Blind Date* theme. It was then, 'Look who's here!' It turned out that they were doing the chanting for the benefit of a newspaper reporter who had a recorder with him and was interviewing some of the would-be, hopefully, stars of a show. It had happened to me on my first audition, a local reporter asking some of us what inspired us to go in for it. I can recall saying that it was just for a bit of fun. No doubt some of these had the same thought, although one girl confided to me that she was looking for a husband. Good luck to her, I thought, you never know, we needed some more members of the exclusive club.

Neil, one of the researchers, popped his head out of the next room to see what all the fuss was about and said, 'Oh! It's you!'

Now, where had I heard that remark before? He told us that Thelma (the Producer) was due back shortly, and that he would send her in saying that two people wanted to see her.

It was great to talk to those people, and to encourage them to give their best. We should know that, because competition is strong, the prize is worth the effort. When Thelma came into the room, first of all she didn't see Lilian, but looked right over the top of her head, as she was sitting down. Well, I'm not surprised, really, Lilian's not very tall even when she's standing up. Not that in any way this remark can be construed as a criticism of my Lilian, bless her little cotton socks!

Joking aside, Thelma was pleased to see us and had time for a coffee and a chat. We left and returned later with a gift for the *Blind Date* office, well, for the team, really, a china ornament depicting a bride and groom, symbolic of the ultimate achievement, for Thelma to take back with her.

Whilst in Liverpool we visited a couple of outdoor markets and the largest car boot sale that I had ever seen. It was in a multi-storey car park, on every floor, and it took ages to get round. Many of the traders called out, 'Where's Cilla?' to which we usually replied, 'She'll be along in a minute.' It is of course Cilla's home town, they love her there, and it shows in their remarks. She's their champion.

The next visit was to a huge indoor market, held in a massive disused warehouse, row upon row of stalls, some even converted into shops, selling everything imaginable. It was well worth a visit, and Lilian was in her element. Upstairs was a café, selling the usual sandwiches, coffee and tea and snacks. It's thirsty and hungry work trudging around, so what better than a little light sustenance? Having received my order, I proffered my money, only to have it handed back by the proprietor, saying,

'No charge, we don't often get celebrities in here. After all, you were on television with our Cilla!' So you can see what I meant about how they feel about her. I was about four quid better off too.

We had been to two more auditions, one in Bristol, where we had lunch with the team, and one in Taunton, when we had coffee with Nina. The latter one being the scene of my original audition. We had mentioned to Chris at LWT that we would like to sit in the audience at one of the shows, so he sent us two tickets. These tickets are free on application to LWT, but children under fifteen are not admitted.

We queued at the audience entrance, and were shown to our seats, which had been reserved. Ted Robbins, in his warm up, introduced us. We had a great reception from the team members who were present. Then Cilla came in for a pre-show appearance and a chat with the audience, and we were very pleased when she spoke to Lilian and I, asking how the marriage was, and saying she would see us after the show.

That was our first experience of the show from the spectators' gallery, and hopefully not the last. We were invited to cheer and clap and show our appreciation of the contestants' efforts, and it was great fun. We look forward to the next one with great anticipation.

Quite a few of our relatives and friends have told us of different incidents, especially abroad. When asked where they lived, they would reply, 'Hemyock, in Devon,' to be answered by, 'Isn't that where the *Blind Date* couple comes from?' I admit that until eleven years ago, when my daughter and her family moved to Devon, I had not heard of Hemyock, but, come to think of it, there are probably more villages in the UK that I have not heard of, than those that I have, so it is not surprising really. I'm getting a bit out of my depth here, perhaps some day they might stick a piece of stone in the wall inscribed *Lilian and David, the Blind Date couple, lived here.* Well, they might, especially if I carve it myself.

One of the first official functions we were asked to perform was at the local preparatory school, when we were asked if we would judge the children's Easter efforts in model making. One had to start somewhere, and where better than in our own village?

Another was the opening of a charity shop in Taunton, a 'Save the Children' shop, with a limited opening before Christmas.

There were two more, both in Jersey, which are mentioned in earlier chapters, and just recently, we were asked to perform the opening ceremony of a Vintage car rally and Village fayre in Thorverton, near Exeter. This was quite an event. Our friends who supplied the complimentary wedding cars for our wedding offered to take us in style in one of their great cars. So with Robin wearing his chauffeur's cap, we arrived, his car attracting a lot of admiring attention. Lilian did a *you've been framed* act by falling flat on her face when she got out of the car, but apart from a few minor cuts and bruises she was not damaged, I was pleased to know. Really, I couldn't catch her, I got out of the other door! The ribbon was stretched between two snorting steam tractors, Lilian cut it, both tractors blew their steam whistles and I was nearly a father. We were treated to an excellent lunch by our hosts.

We attended a television morning show by John Stapleton, entitled *The Time, The Place*, the theme being 'beards'. We had telephoned in our views on the subject, principally because Lilian had expressed her dislike for beards when she had picked me on the show, and Cilla had said to her, 'Get him to shave it off, chuck.' So we had an interesting contribution to make to the show. I still have the beard, however, so it can't be that bad.

I have not mentioned the pantomimes that we attended during the year. There was the *Robinson Crusoe* panto at the Pavilion theatre, Bournemouth, where Buster Merryfield was appearing as Captain Cockle. We had our photograph taken with him in his panto outfit, copies of which appeared in the local papers, *The Bournemouth Echo*, and the *Advertiser*. There were many stars that we had the pleasure to be introduced to after attending their shows, including Windsor Davies, Tessa Sanderson, The Krankies, 'Trojan' from the Gladiators, Matthew Kelly, Chris Akabusi, Lorraine Chase, Rosemary Ford, Jeff Holland and Anne Charleston (Madge from *Neighbours*). It was our pleasure whilst in Bournemouth and staying at Sandbanks where we had a commanding view of all vessels entering and leaving Poole Harbour, to visit the Bournemouth International Centre to see two shows. One, the *Russ Abbott Summer Spectacular* with Russ, Bella Emberg and Gary Lovini, a super violinist. A really good show with lots of laughs. The other was the *Magic of the Musicals*, starring Jacqui Scott and Mark Rattray. These two great singing stars we had the pleasure of meeting after their show. Last, I need to talk about the future. There are a few things lined up, a holiday in Bournemouth (What? Not again?) but yes we are away for a week, then on to a Golden Wedding celebration of a WAAF and her husband who shared the same RAF camp during the war years. The following day we are off to another Golden Wedding celebration, this time for my brother Harry, who incidentally was one of the original war time code breakers (Ssh!). My Brother was responsible for the installation of the first Electronic Computer in the World, named COLOSSUS. He was later one of the designers of E.R.N.I.E., and at present he is helping to re-build Colossus at Bletchley Park, where it is on view to the public.

After leaving Bournemouth we travelled to Kessingland, near Lowestoft, to attend one of the Golden Wedding Anniversaries referred to.

There was a 3 WAAF (I should say ex WAAF) reunion incorporated in the festivities, Lilian being one of them. They obviously had a lot to talk about, and mainly, I gathered, about the various friends and acquaintances of that bygone time, the details of which I haven't the faintest idea, perhaps it's just as well that I don't. Friend Gladys Recas, at seventy five is a real character: she kept all the guests in stitches, and she runs a club called the 'Kessis'. Somebody had brought along her props, and she gave her rendering of *The Toreador* song, followed by *My old man said follow the van*. It was a great evening, and our congratulations went to Gladys and Fred for their 50 happy years together. Our regards to your relatives who came over from Jamaica and the U.S.A. The following day we travelled to Felixstowe for the Golden Wedding celebration of my Brother Harry and wife. This was a family reunion: from as far as Singapore they came (where we have a standing invitation for a holiday) and relatives whom I had not seen for 30 years or more were there. They were all pleased to meet Lilian, and it marked another memorable occasion. Next, home to Devon, to prepare for our visit to Jersey.

So far as we are aware at present there are three open months with nothing planned until December. I had mentioned earlier that we were going on another cruise, well, we booked through Bolsover Travel a Caribbean cruise on the Canberra, embracing Christmas and New Year. So while the majority of you will be enjoying your Christmas pud at home, we will be having ours at sea, and, wait for it, we are not doing the washing up!

I have been told repeatedly by a number of people that they won't buy this book unless their names appear in it, well, I'm sorry but I can't do this, not even for you, Peter Ferrari!

To sum all this up to date, you may be thinking that Lilian and I are two very lucky people.

We would certainly agree with you on this point, we have no illusions about that, and accept that good fortune has been kind to us. When you read the list of acknowledgements you will understand that we owe our experiences to a lot of individuals and organisations. To those whom we owe a debt of gratitude, and whose names do not appear on this list, nevertheless we know who they are, and to all of them we convey our sincere thanks.

Many people, on their paths through life, say 'I could write a book', well, we said this, and we have done it. It is, as we have already stated, a true story, but it is not the end, it is a phase, yes, a truly remarkable phase in both of our lives, which we ourselves consider worthy of publication, that you, the reader may share in our happiness. But life goes on regardless, we have no intention of standing still, but so long as we are able, we will continue to enjoy the fruits of our experiences.

We hope you have as much enjoyment reading all this, as we have had writing it. God Bless!

Love, love changes everything.